"It's hard to imagine a [   ] the extraordinary life of the [   ] Zack Eswine's *The Imperfect* [   ] ...ore insight into the perils and joys of eve[   ] ...stry in the local church—a refreshingly honest and beautifully written meditation."

   Mark Galli, Editor-in-Chief, *Christianity Today*

"I wish I'd read this book twenty-five years ago when I first began to consider pastoral ministry. The ground Zack covers is vital for novices and senior pastors alike. He steers us well clear of dangerous ambitions, absurd expectations, and corrosive work patterns. But he does so with wit, self-deprecation, and deeply felt realism. Eswine reignited in me a love for the Perfect Shepherd, who has the extraordinary grace to include imperfect shepherds in his kingdom work. This should be on everyone's must-read list!"

   Mark Meynell, Associate Director (Europe), Langham Preaching;
   author, *A Wilderness of Mirrors*

"Zack Eswine has done it again. In *The Imperfect Pastor*, he extends the hand of brotherhood to every minister of the gospel. Too many weary soldiers guard the front lines; Eswine reminds us all that Christ is our guard and defender, and that strength in him is our strongest place."

   Lore Ferguson, writer; graphic designer; speaker

"This book needs to be read by every pastor, to rescue us and call us back to what matters. The expectation of large, famous, and fast ministry in a post-Christian culture can be a destructive burden. Zack's wisdom is a healing balm bringing needed grace to help us minister with patience and endurance."

   Peter Boyd, Pastor, Shore Presbyterian Church, Auckland, New Zealand

"This is simply the best book on pastoral ministry I have ever read. In an upside-down ministry world that idolizes stardom and size, Zack opens our eyes to the only things that really matter. Prayerfully read and reread this beautiful, poignant meditation, and you will discover joy and true greatness in the midst of your extraordinary, ordinary life."

   Ken Shigematsu, Pastor, Tenth Church Vancouver; best-selling author,
   God in My Everything

"Here is wisdom reminiscent of the gifted preachers of another era but expressed in the sound and tone of today. Here is pastoral theology written, preached, and lived out in the very real and checkered life of Zack himself. Here is humane and godly counsel. You should read this book!"

   Leighton Ford, President, Leighton Ford Ministries

The Imperfect Pastor

The Imperfect Pastor

Discovering Joy in Our Limitations through
a Daily Apprenticeship with Jesus

Zack Eswine

WHEATON, ILLINOIS

Trade paperback ISBN: 978-1-4335-4933-5
ePub ISBN: 978-1-4335-4936-6
PDF ISBN: 978-1-4335-4934-2
Mobipocket ISBN: 978-1-4335-4935-9

Library of Congress Cataloging-in-Publication Data
Eswine, Zack, 1969–
   The imperfect pastor : discovering joy in our
limitations through a daily apprenticeship with Jesus /
Zack Eswine.
      pages cm
   Includes bibliographical references and index.
   ISBN 978-1-4335-4933-5 (tp)
   1. Pastoral theology. I. Title.
BV4011.3.E89   2015
253—dc23   2015011196

Crossway is a publishing ministry of Good News Publishers.

VP	25	24	23	22	21	20	19	18	17
15	14	13	12	11	10	9	8	7	6	5	4

For Mamaw, Papaw, and Jessica
I look forward to introducing you

Contents

Acknowledgments

I want to thank Dave DeWit, whose heart for leaders in ministry and commitment to this book have humbled and encouraged me. Thanks also to Lydia Brownback for editing.

I'm grateful to Bruwer Vroon, Matt Blazer, and the elders of Riverside Church for reading drafts and making suggestions. Thank you, Jessica, for all of your late-night and Saturday readings. Your insights, suggestions, and encouragement in our partnership together bless me.

I am grateful for Riverside Church, out of whose life together in our daily and ordinary ways I write this book.

Introduction

I became a pastor. But I didn't know how to be one.

    The Serpent saw this. He seized his opportunity.

    "You can be like God," he said. And I, the fool, believed him.

    Looking back over these twenty years of pastoral work, the words of a poet come to mind. They set the stage for conversation I'd like to have with you.

> Chances are, the preacher reasons,
> You'll be more willing to listen
> Now that your city has fallen from what it was.[1]

I'm listening more. I invite you in your fallen city to join me.

    When I started, I did not know that a pastoral vocation in Jesus would limit me, slow me down, and painfully undo the misguided mentoring of my life. Now, I know that my success and joy as a pastor depend upon this.

    So do yours.

    The book you hold in your hands is, in some measure, an up-dated—and shortened—rewrite of my earlier work *Sensing Jesus*. I hesitated when I was invited to rewrite the earlier volume. Like any writer, I contemplated the loss of prized sentences, and I flinched. But now I give thanks for the opportunity and the effort. This new work, *The Imperfect Pastor*, is half the size of *Sensing Jesus*; nevertheless, one-third of the content is brand-new. *Sensing Jesus* will find its place in used bookstores and academic libraries, while *The Imperfect Pastor* will stand on its own with distinct language, size, content, and purpose. I hope that in its pages you will find the grace of Jesus for your life and ministry.

PART ONE

The Calling We Pursue

Vocation

The place He gives us to inhabit.
The few things He gives us to do in that place.
The persons He invites us to know there.
These our days,
our lingering.

It is enough then,
this old work of hands
His and ours
to love here,
to learn His song here,

like crickets that scratch
and croon,
from nooks unseen,

carrying on with
what they were made for,
the night craft of
unnoticed faces,
with our wings unobserved,

until He walks again
in the cool of the day,
to reclaim our names.

And we then,
with our stitched white flags,
will from behind His evergreens,
finally unhide ourselves
and with Him
we will stroll once more.

1

Desire

He thinks only of what he wants and he does not ask
himself whether he ought to want it.

BERNARD OF CLAIRVAUX

I remember sitting out on the carport at a picnic table at my grand-
parents' house in Henryville, Indiana. I was in the third year of
my first pastorate. I had taken a brief study leave to write my first
article for a ministry journal. Mamaw, glad for my extended visit,
made the spice cake she always made when I came to town. As I
took up my pen and looked down Lake Road, I felt what any person surely feels when he gets to do something that he knows he was
made to do—that noble pleasure of feeling that somehow we are
enough for the day, that the day cannot contain us because we will
outshine it. In my case, I felt a growing desire to write something of
significance for pastors. I wanted it to be exceptional.

That sabbatical week I devoured the subject that thrilled me
most at the time—early Princeton Seminary and preaching. This
probably sounds annoying or incredibly boring to some. But to
me the subject was like Mamaw's spice cake. The first principal
of Princeton, Archibald Alexander, and his son seemed to have so
much to say that fed my soul about preaching. It offered delight-

ful food for the wounded pastor I was becoming. Looking back, it sobers me to realize how new I was in ministry, yet how deeply tired I was already.

But somehow, the feeling that we are doing something significant can enable us to tell ourselves that things are not as bad as they seem. A good memory can likewise join this feeling. Together they can fuel a respite of hope. Dr. Calhoun had regularly shared with me his living room and some tea. Over the months, he had passed his love of old Princeton on to me (and to others). With such a memory joining an opportunity to write and Mamaw's spice cake right in front of me, I felt energized. I had always hoped to change the world. I desired to.

Looking back now, I thought this kind of desire was made for an epic or grand moment. (Exceptional persons are not bound to a life of unexceptional moments, right?) Such epic moments when realized would leave nothing the same. Heaven itself will have touched us. This idea of a grand swoop flirted with my desires. The epic aspiration began to hold hands with my attempts to preach.

I was not alone in this. My colleagues with whom I graduated from seminary shared these cravings and dreams. Nor was this unreasonable in my mind. After all, my professors and my fellow students publicly recognized my preaching and affirmed these gifts. I had also read of how God attended preachers with his Spirit in the past, and I desired that he might do so with us in the present. But two years into my first church, all my preaching seemed to do at the time was give a lot of people cause for checking out other churches.

So I began to desire finding an epic moment outside the pulpit. I'd try to pastor people to this grand end. But the level of strife that existed among my elders confounded me. I was hitting that stretch of highway in the desert that most new pastors must drive through in the first two to four years at a new call—the desert when most of us bail out. But I didn't realize that then. Nor did I realize the large brokenness a little church can muster. At the time, I did not understand what I now feel compelled to tell you. Pastors are no different from anybody. We too can get "lost in our longings."[1]

Desire

The Serpent knows this. The trees in the garden were desirable, good, and pleasant (Gen. 2:9). But when Eve saw the one tree, she craved it in a way that was bent. She and Adam sought to consume it apart from God and in spite of his stated purpose for that tree (Gen. 3:6). They pined for a desirable thing but in all the wrong ways. We can do this with ministry too.

Make no mistake. Desire is a firework. Handled wisely it fills the night sky with light, color, beauty, and delight. Handle desire poorly, and it can burn your neighborhood down (James 4:1–2).

I know firsthand about the beauty and arson of ministerial desires. I know what it is to get lost in these desires and to need finding again in Jesus. I was one of those guys to whom people would say, "You are among the finest preachers I have heard, and you are so young. I can't wait to hear you in ten years." Well, ten years have long since passed, and I have not become what was once projected.

I do not mean this morbidly. I hope you will soon see that I am writing to you as one who feels profoundly rescued from himself by the abounding grace of Jesus. But the stale waters of celebrity, consumerism, and immediate gratification had infiltrated my drinking water. My pastoral desires had become tainted, and I did not realize it. A lot of us don't. We and our congregations suffer for it.

So let's establish the fact that pastoral vocation begins with desire. The apostle Paul says as much:

> The saying is trustworthy: If anyone *aspires* to the office of overseer, he *desires* a noble task. (1 Tim. 3:1)

Peter agrees: "Shepherd the flock of God that is among you, exercising oversight," he says. "not under compulsion, but *willingly*" (1 Pet. 5:2).

Reflect with me for a moment if you can. When did you first make your desire for the ministry known? Were you older or younger? Who did you tell? For me, I was in second grade at Saint Anthony's Elementary School. Mrs. Canter had written a question on the chalkboard: "What do you want to be when you grow up?" I answered, and Mrs. Canter patched two words together in chalk for all to see: "Zack—Priest."

I had not yet associated pastoral desire with the love of money (Luke 16:14), networking for position (Matt. 23:6–7), the lust for power (Acts 8:18–21), or the advancement of my own name. I did not know yet that serving God could be used, even by me, as means to try, in line with the Serpent's old whisper, to become like God (Gen. 3:5). All I knew as an eight-year-old was that I desired to serve God with my life in vocational ministry. I wasn't restless then, not at all. It was marvelous.

Since then, I've learned something, though not as a priest it turns out, but as a pastor. There are many kinds of desires at work in this world, and not all of them are kind.

What If You're an Unnamed Mountain?

My desires began to run after the wrong kind of mentoring. I interned as a youth pastor at a small church, the place of my beginnings of pastoral ministry. My pastor spent hours and hours mentoring me for three years. But I noticed something. As we walked into regular regional gatherings of pastors and church leaders, he and I entered quietly while other pastors periodically entered the room to a kind of fanfare. They were the large-church pastors. Some of them had written books, moderated assemblies, and preached for thousands. Though years later I would know something of that kind of fanfare, my faithful mentoring pastor never would.

Along the way, I found out some of the reasons why. I was part of a team that offered an annual conference for pastors. The year we tried to resist a celebrity mind-set, we barely funded the conference. Our speakers were longtime, veteran ministry leaders who were nonetheless unknown. The registration for the conference was woeful.

The next year we returned to getting big names so people would come. Sure enough, it was packed. In our land, a pastor's experience and wisdom have little monetary value unless we know his name. Where did that idea come from? I don't know. But take note. The message was loud and clear for me as a young minister in training.

I'm trying to tell you that by the time I was twenty-six and finishing seminary, the purity of my second-grade desire to serve God for his own sake was fading, and I knew it. It was becoming quite clear to me that if I was to prove successful in ministry, I needed to do something great, and I needed to define something great in terms of how large, famous, and fast I could accomplish it.

Looking back on those early introductions to pastoral culture, an anecdote shared between the famed Richard Foster and his son, Nathan, now comes to mind. Nathan was eager to quickly conquer the famous mountains of Colorado. While resting on the rocky side of one of those celebrity mountains, Richard pointed his son to the beauty of an adjacent mountain:

> Nate, see that mountain? It has a stunning ridge. That's a perfectly good peak. If it stood a few feet higher, you would know its name and want to climb it. As it stands, it's an unnamed mountain that no one bothers with.[2]

Desiring to Do a Great Thing for God

So by the time I was in the third year of my first pastorate, eating spice cake on Mamaw's porch, I was growing increasingly restless. Like many of my colleagues, I craved making an epic difference for God in my vocation as fast as possible. Contrast the synonyms for *ordinary* with the synonyms for *epic*, and who can blame us?

> I aspire to serve as a common, ordinary, mundane, normal, routine, average, usual, and humdrum pastor for an unexceptional,

commonplace, everyday, run-of-the-mill congregation. As a preacher I am unremarkable and middling.

Or:

I aspire to serve as an Olympian, uncommon, surpassing, extraordinary, special pastor for a marvelous, remarkable, singular, exceedingly great congregation. As a preacher I am stellar and unforgettable.

I felt anything but stellar. *Maybe this article is just the beginning,* I thought. *I'm not an epic pastor or preacher. But maybe I could write what just might change the world for God.*

That was twenty years ago. I did publish that article, but I still had to brush my teeth the next day. In the years since, I've seen people come to saving faith in Jesus, marriages healed, addictions overcome. I've traveled, preached, gotten a PhD, taught, counseled, and written books. Jesus has revealed himself so kindly, truly, presently, and powerfully. But as I mentioned, there is beauty and arson in desire. Of those attending my ordination to the ministry those years ago, one pastor mentor took his own life, and another is no longer in the ministry due to moral misconduct. One elder and one deacon were painfully disciplined, one for raging mistreatment and the other for a devastating affair. Other friendships eventually gave way amid the ugly politics of ministry. And twelve years after my public vow to gospel ministry, my marriage ended. The only thing large, famous, and fast about me and much of my ministerial crowd is our brokenness.

When I spoke desire for ministry in Mrs. Canter's second-grade class, I would never have imagined that my future would require me to learn to do life as a single dad with primary care of my three children amid a community of "scandal" and rumor. I've had to take a long, hard look in the mirror of my own tainted desires. I'm asking you to do the same in hopes of sparing you the cost I've paid. Being declared "innocent in the matter" didn't remove the whispers or the slanders either in the community or in my own head. Neither did these remove what it meant for each of my three children and me to daily learn together to see the sun again and smile. But take note, in case you now believe that you are not like me. I've also had to examine those who projected what I was "supposed" to become in their eyes in ten years' time. You will have to contend with this too. We have to take a hard look at the "large things famously and fast" desire that congregational members and pastoral constituencies seem constantly to yearn for. The absence of our attentiveness to these misfired desires is making us a ragged bunch.

So now here I sit, all these years later, typing these words as pastor of a little church in Missouri. An irony whispers to my thoughts. I am hoping that what I write to you now will prove significant. I shake my head and almost laugh—that short exhale of a laugh through the nose. Funny how I once thought that significance lay somewhere beyond Henryville and Mamaw's presence—a local place and an ordinary love—as if an article in a journal or a pulpit sermon would do more to glorify God in my generation than attending faithfully to either of these other created gifts of his.

Conversations with a Young Pastor

In this light, listen in for a moment. Years later, on the other side of the ruins, I found myself listening to a young pastor's desires. I saw and heard myself in him. Maybe you will too.

"No matter what, I want to go all out for the ministry," he said.

His passion inspired me, but the context worried me. We had just spoken at length about his difficulty as a husband and father along with a recurring bend within the road of his soul. I took a breath and paused, staring down at the bowl of pad thai in front of me.

"If the ministry is what we will go all out for," I began, "then how we define 'the ministry' seems important, you know?" I took a bite and chewed.

"I just want to preach the Word," he declared. "No matter what happens, as long as I keep saying what God said, he will bless it. I know God has given me purpose."

There was urgency in his voice, hurry in his eyes. Both were like a mirror to me. I twirled peanut and noodles around my fork (the chopsticks had long ago begun their humbling work with me). I was hunting for words.

"Yes, God will bless his Word," I ventured. "You do have purpose," I affirmed.

I lingered more with the bowl, trying to find what to leave unsaid. "I spoke at a conference once," I began. "I preached five times. It was one of those moments when God's presence was tangibly felt. In fact, after that particular conference, the rest of my year was planned full with preaching all over the country. God does bless his Word. I've seen him do it firsthand."

"But," I said, and then stopped. I stood at a crossroads in my mind, wondering how to say what was next. "On my way home after that last sermon amid the divine blessing of that night, my wife of fifteen years told me she was leaving me."

There was a quiet between my young friend and me. I sipped my Coke. I was afraid I'd said too much too soon. He knew the circumstances of my life. But was he ready to learn something of what such circumstances might have to teach us? Moreover, was I ready to try and give some kind of voice to it?

"I'm trying to suggest," I said, "that 'the ministry' involves more than the question of whether our sermons are powerful and we influence crowds of people. Going all out for God means more than going all out for sermons and crowds."

Later that night we stood beneath the stars.

"When I get back home," he said, "I finally begin as a pastor. Maybe soon I can get to seminary and get equipped and then become a professor somewhere. I can't wait to get there. Two years as a pastor and then . . ."

I found myself staring at the gravel driveway like it was a bowl of pad thai. I searched again for what to leave unsaid. I heard my voice in his. He was restless to do something great for God. His pastoral work was a platform to use to help him get somewhere other than where he was. And yet he did not know how to include changing diapers or holding his wife's hand in his definition of greatness.

"What if you are there already?" I tried. "I mean, what if you are already what God has in mind for you? You are a blessing to people in Jesus already. What if the place of ministry where you are with the family that you have is the place where God means for you to be with him?"

His face seemed pained.

"Please forgive me if I'm saying too much," I said. Then I paused. "It's just that you are talking to a man," I mustered, "who got everything he dreamed of and lost most of what really mattered, and all of this in the name of going all out for the ministry and serving God. I'm just trying to say that it seems really important to know what we mean by 'the ministry' if we are going to go all out for it. My desire is that what you are going all out for is actually the thing God intends with the definition God gives it."

He looked away into the sky again. "I don't know where to start with all that," he protested.

Homeless in Our Living Rooms

The following week, I sat for lunch with an up-and-coming pastor. The church he served was only four years old but had several hundred already in attendance. He was rising in our community as the next big thing.

Yet there was something troubling him. "The first two years of our explosive growth," he admitted, "I related poorly as a husband and father." He stared into his ice water and grimaced. "I hid in my success as a pastor," he continued. "I think I used it to avoid my failing ways at home and in my heart."

This man was the epitome of what my younger friend was striving to be. But both men revealed the same struggle—the realization that one can receive accolades for preaching Jesus, yet at the same time know very little about how to follow Jesus in the living rooms of their ordinary lives. They could communicate love to a crowd from the pulpit or in an office or a classroom, but when called upon to give themselves (and not their gifts), they were fumble prone. I see this in me.

My young friend wrote to me during the first week in his new pastorate:

> I am full of anxiety, mostly about what I do with all this time. I keep asking myself, have I done X-number of dollars of labor for the church today? I am unaccustomed to this free of a day, and it makes me anxious. I get things done better when my schedule is packed and I'm going a million miles an hour. I've known nothing but pressure for years, and now that God is providing space, I want to sabotage it somehow. How can I turn from this and find life?

My friend did not know how to do a pastor's day if efficiency, quantity, speed, and economic measures were removed from him. He hadn't been taught about the other kinds of treasures that were his in Jesus and that he could desire for use in his day. Me neither. His time with me over the years hadn't helped him.

Desire, Haste, and the "Mattering Things"

But I hope by pains that you and I could help him now. We could say something like this, couldn't we?

> As you enter ministry, you will be tempted to orient your desires toward doing large things in famous ways as fast and as efficiently as you can. But take note. A crossroads waits for you. Jesus is that crossroads. Because almost anything in life that truly matters will require you to do small, mostly overlooked things, over a long period of time with him. The pastoral vocation, because it focuses on helping people cultivate what truly matters, is therefore no exception.

Why? What are these mattering things, meant for our desires? Well, first, love for God. This noble desire takes time. Forgiveness; reconciliation; coming to our senses; spiritual growth in faith, hope, and love; knowledge of and surrender to the teachings of Scripture in Jesus; growing in obedience, gentleness, peace, patience, kindness, and self-control; along with facing addictions, idolatries, and sins with the gospel; learning contentment in Jesus whether we abound or are desolate; waiting for the coming of the Lord and his kingdom and the fulfillment of all God's promises for his glory and our good. The finish line for satisfying these desires can't be crossed with a forty-yard dash, no matter how furiously we try.

Second, love for others in their delights also matters, and this likewise takes time. Learning how to walk and talk and count, growing up, doing math, being able to drive or be on one's own, along with starting or joining a church or ministry. Hurry cannot accomplish such things, much less remaining single, finding true friendship, thriving in marriage, making satisfying love, parenting, grandparenting, or creating integrity and reputation at your job. Learning how to play an instrument, rising to the top in a sport, or becoming expert at a craft or trade doesn't happen overnight. But many people you minister to believe that this kind of love for God and neighbor is supposed to happen instantly.

Take an exasperated husband, for example. He said to me, "I just can't take this; it's too much! Either she deals with this issue, or it's obvious that she doesn't care about this marriage! I'm not going to put up with it anymore!"

When he said this to me, he had been married a total of three months. The issue he referred to was six days old. He quoted the Bible and talked in epic terms about what God wants for a marriage and a life. Yet if he had to wait six days to fix this issue in the context of having been married for a total of eighty-nine days, it was obvious to him that God was not in the marriage or that his wife didn't love him, and that he had to prepare to move on. This man can quote the Bible, but he has no stamina to wait upon God amid something that he does not like. For all the grand talk about stellar things that God wants, it does not occur to him how grand a thing God says it is to learn how to persevere and wait upon him. Many of us pastors express the same kind of emotional inability to wait on God in and for our congregations.

Our problem is that most of the God-given joys we seek get damaged when words like *instantly* and *haste* and *impatience* are thrown at us. Many of us are confused about what it means to have true joy if we have to embrace a delayed gratification amid the slower speeds required by the things that most matter to Jesus.

Now imagine loving God and others through the desolations of life. Desolation cannot easily endure an accelerated pastoral pace. This explains why many of us have no patience for pastoral care. Broken bones and minds are not hurry prone. Burned skin or victimized souls have to get to the miserable itching in order to heal, and we who wait by the bedside must wait some more. Death, grief, loss, recovery from addiction, as well as emotional or physical trauma, parenting special-needs kids, adjusting to chronic illness, depression, disability, or disease—all of these desolations are handled poorly when "efficiency" and "quantitative measures" are required of them. To the important pastor doing large and famous things speedily, the brokenness of people actually feels like an intrusion keeping us from getting our important work for God done. I write that last sentence, and it undoes me. Reread it. Then fall with me, won't you? Fall to your knees with me before the Savior. He is the lifter of our heads. We need this gracious lifting, for we haven't even spoken yet of how words like *instant* and *impatient* offer us no resources to handle the mattering thing of loving our enemies in ministry. And make no mistake: eventually you will have to learn this hardest of neighbor loves too.

As a rule then (and this often surprises us), haste is no friend to desire. The wise man says so, because "whoever makes haste with his feet misses his way" (Prov. 19:2). His point is clear enough. Haste has a habit of not coming through on things that truly matter.

In a crisis it can help. But when it comes to understanding, sorting out, and fulfilling the desires of a human soul, haste constantly and legitimately gets sued for malpractice. Haste offers immediate promises to our desires for a mate or ministry or work or our kids, but haste actually can never deliver on these promises for what is most precious to us.

The point I'm now making is this. Our desire for greatness in ministry isn't the problem. Our problem rises from how the haste of doing large things, famously and as fast as we can, is reshaping our definition of what a great thing is. Desire greatness, dear pastor! But bend your definition of greatness to the one Jesus gives us. At minimum we must begin to take a stand on this one important fact: obscurity and greatness are not opposites.

What Do You Want Jesus to Do for You?

Jesus poses the question of desire so plainly in his training of ministers. "What do you want me to do for you?" he asks (Mark 10:36).

Pause here for a moment. Slow down if you can. Do you have a bucket list for ministry, all the great ministry achievements you want to accomplish in his name before you die? You would not be alone if you did. Just read the classified ads, and myriad desires of those who make up your congregation and community reveal themselves too.

James and John had bucket lists. "We want you to do for us whatever we ask of you," they said. "Grant us to sit, one at your right hand and one at your left, in your glory" (Mark 10:35–37).

James and John had begun to subtly yearn that their ministry with Jesus would provide them a platform for greatness. Their cravings began to wreck their community (Mark 10:41). Jesus did not stop this friction or potential wreckage from happening. He still doesn't. Did you mark that down? James and John were dearly loved, gifted, called, fruitful, and central to Jesus's earthly ministry. He graciously heard their desires. But their closeness to Jesus and their fruitfulness in ministry didn't mean that everything they did, said, or craved was blessed by God, or that everything they did was good, right, and helpful to those who knew them.

Instead of giving them such immunity, Jesus responded. What he says sobers us. It is possible for ministry leaders to desire greatness in ways no different from anyone, anywhere in our culture. Attaching Jesus's name to these desires doesn't change the fact that they look just like the cravings of the world.

Pause here. Read that last sentence again if you need to. Prayerfully slow down for this. Human leaders everywhere desire greatness and to lord it over others. "It shall not be so among you," Jesus declared. If it is greatness that you desire, you must from now on surrender your life to greatness of a different kind. "Whoever would be great among you must be your servant" (Mark 10:43). Servants give their days to small, mostly overlooked tasks over long periods of time with no accolade.

Jesus then takes James, John, and his other students in ministry into a living case study. He shows them an unnamed mountain of a man. This man was poor and blind. Jesus offers this poor orb-shattered man the same powerful question that he gave to those who were a "big deal" and traveled with him: "What do you want me to do for you?" (Mark 10:51).

Right here, the grace of Jesus humbles us in the contrast of desires he unearths. James and John were in the thick of ministry with Jesus and among Jesus's prized pupils. Yet this was not enough for them. They wanted better seats. Meanwhile, the poor man asked Jesus only for two things, and the first thing was mercy. The second was sight.

I think back to Mrs. Canter's class, my seminary internship, my first pastorate, Mamaw's porch, and the shattered remains of my ministerial crowd. When did it happen in my ambitions for ministry that I no longer felt my need to desire mercy when with Jesus? When did I begin to presume upon the privilege of my eyes working properly and define greatness from the vantage point of my privilege rather than the vantage point of Jesus's grace?

There is a way of desiring to go all out for the ministry that will split you in two, cause pain to those you serve, and reveal how far off from Jesus's definition of greatness you've drifted. I know this firsthand. But I'm learning something else too. There is more grace and more hope here than you may yet know—a vocation of pastoral work among the greatness of slow, overlooked people and places can become in God's hands, all gift, true joy, abiding contentment, and good life. Why? Because this is Jesus's way. Where Jesus is our portion and desire, we lack no true treasure.

> The kingdom of heaven is like treasure hidden in a field, which a man found and covered up. Then in his joy he goes and sells all that he has and buys that field. (Matt. 13:44)

Could it be that joyfully selling all we have includes letting go of our misguided ministry bucket lists? What if the joy we desire in Jesus is like hidden treasure in a field that many people, even in ministry, overlook and rarely buy?

Do you remember what it was like before you desired vocational ministry? You had no training. You were unknown in the world. Jesus was lovely to you. He had saved you. He had communicated his love to you. He was all treasure, true, pleasurable, satisfying, and altogether beautiful. He was your portion. He was your desire. It was this ravishing provision of Jesus that roused your affections to serve him in the first place with your life in vocational ministry. No wonder, when Peter declared that he would excel and outdo all his ministry colleagues, the rooster's crow wasn't long in coming. To restore Peter to ministry, Jesus took Peter all the way back to first things, first loves. "Peter, do you love me? Then feed my sheep" (see John 21:15–17). This is where our vocation begins. Pastoral calling to feed others is secondary to and flows out of a prior desire for the loveliness of Jesus himself. The old hymn comes to mind: "Prone to wander, Lord, I feel it, prone to leave the God I love." But Peter learned what we all do in the ashes of ministerial rooster crows. Jesus comes for us. He hasn't left us. His steadfast love endures forever.

Conclusion

Let's close this introductory conversation about pastoral desire with this real-life parable.

Two men left home to plant a church in a city of need. The first one to arrive dreamed of a city reached for Jesus with the gospel. Through this first pastor, people came to know Jesus, believers gathered, and a community of Jesus followers was born. It was a slow work, but it was happening. His prayers were being answered.

In time, he began to meet with the second one, at the time a church planter. He did so to encourage this second pastor in his fledgling work. The old-timer and the newcomer prayed for Jesus to reach the city. Through the newcomer, people came to know Jesus, believers gathered, and a community of Jesus followers was born.

Ten years later, the one who had come first serves as pastor of an "ordinary" church. Its two hundred–plus members demonstrate the love of Jesus in ways that did not exist there ten years earlier. The newcomer who came second pastors an "epic" church. Its thousands of members and multiple sites around the city demonstrate the love of Jesus in ways that did not exist there ten years earlier. The prayers of both men were answered.

Why then is one of them sad?

Why then does only one of them receive our invitations to speak at our conferences and give us advice?

2

Recovering Our Humanity

We have no home in this world, I used to say, and then I'd walk back up the road to this old place and make myself a pot of coffee and a fried-egg sandwich.

MARILYNNE ROBINSON

"You can be like God," the Serpent says.

"But how?" I ask.

I read the Bible with glasses.

I kneel to pray for people with coffee breath.

I stand to preach Jesus with a blister on my foot.

I serve the Lord's Supper with bread bought for $1.99 at Schnuck's Grocery.

"Just pretend it is otherwise," the Snake responds. "People love it that way."

Advice for a Would-Be Pastor

I had recently learned that a longtime pastor and personal mentor committed suicide. I took a sabbatical from the seminary where I served as professor and spent six months as interim pastor with my departed friend's family and congregation. I had pastored a church before. I had served as an interim before. But not like this. We would forage together for scraps of grace and truth amid the wreckage. The living Christ would inhabit the heaps with us. We would learn from him in the trash. He would sup with us in the shadow's valley.

But presently I was seated in a crowd of professors and ministry students in our jeans and tennis shoes. I was asked to give a word. What could I say to help a rookie in ministry?

The atmosphere was light, but my heart was heavy. I was thinking about how my pastor mentor could have chosen to step down from ministry and still have mattered to all of us. But for him, stepping down in the midst of inner haunting indicated not humanity but failure. He could not see himself useful if he no longer held the position of pastor with the care for others that the position enabled. I missed him. I was, for the first time in my life, asking myself the same question. Did I know that I could serve Christ humanly and significantly whether or not I was a pastor or leader in ministry? I did not know it at that time, but I would soon have to answer such a question in a painful and public way. For the moment, however, among those ministry students, with grief in my heart and soberly confronting my assumptions about what it meant to lead in ministry, it was now my turn to speak. I breathed a quick prayer and stood. That's when I said it. "Jonathan Edwards farted."

Some laughed. I didn't. Some smirked at my irreverence. Maybe I was irreverent. I wasn't trying to be funny. I probably could have found better language to describe what I was grappling with. I had no intention to disparage the great theologian and pastor from America's history. I was trying to put words to the damage and myth of his celebrity and others'. I felt harassed by a new question in my being: What does it mean for us that if revival came and we went on into the night with heaven-sent prayer, we'd all still have to use the bathroom at some point? I wanted to say that even the greatest theologians or preachers among us are still just

ordinary persons needy for grace in Jesus. I was tired of pretending otherwise.

First Things First

At a conference, I preach Christ for you with a hemorrhoid while
my books are on sale out in the hallway. What is more, I may have
seen myself in my children's eyes that morning and had to ask their
forgiveness for something the day before, or maybe I'm still blind
as I speak to you regarding what my wife or my children or my
congregation still desperately need me to see. When I visit you in
the hospital, I had to tie my shoes that morning or figure out which
sweater makes me look a bit slimmer or cry out to God with my
own doubts as you hurt and I have no answer why. When you've
been changed by grace through something I said or wrote, I likely
had a bowl of oatmeal for breakfast or enjoyed the sound of the
owl that visits our place.

Therefore, as we begin to think about desires, we need to cry
from the rooftops that pastoral ministry is creaturely. A pastor is
a human being. *I believe that Christian life and ministry are an
apprenticeship with Jesus toward recovering our humanity and,
through his Spirit, helping our neighbors do the same.* All of this is
for, through, by, with, and in him for the glory of God.

I also believe that the general absence of this recovery of our
humanity within pastoral ministry is spiritually killing us. I want
something done about it. I realize that placing our humanity in
Christ front and center for the Christian life and the pastoral task
will make some of us uneasy, and rightly so. It could seem that I
intend to droll out only more of the self-centered spirituality that
our generation and our own hearts harmfully want.

To allay such concerns, I think of a professor and friend of mine.
He sometimes has his ministers in training turn individually and
face the rest of the class and confess out loud to the rest, "I am not
the Christ." In these words from John the Baptist, we learn that
while it is true that we can dangerously make too little of God by

drawing improper attention to ourselves, it is equally true that we cannot fully magnify God without confessing that we are not him. To say "I am not the Christ" is simultaneously to expose for all to see that we pastors are merely human and only local.

I use the words *merely* human and *only* local in order to differentiate us from Jesus. Jesus is human, but not *merely*. Jesus is local, but not *only*. We clarify this distinction between Jesus and us as an act of worship and commitment. As ministry leaders we endeavor to give of our lives in such a way that every neighbor we minister to will know that we are not God. Each of us is not God and is only human.

So let's mark this point down. Greatness, even in ministry, cannot escape humanity. Being human does not mar greatness; it informs it and sets its noble boundaries. How have we come to think otherwise? Whatever desire we may crave for ministry, we do so as one whose big toe can itch and whose sockless feet get cold in winter.

Human Physicality

Pastoral desires, however grand or noble, do not deliver us from bodily limits.

Theological study taught me the doctrine of creation. I was examined for ordination on my views of creation days and Darwin's legacy. But what it means that God created us human, bodily, local, finite, and in his image did not translate into my theology of pastoral ministry nor inform the shape that pastoral work must take. I think now that it should.

For example, I am one of Wendell's pastors. Polio has held Wendell's legs hostage for seventy years. Wendell has conformed to the regimen of diabetes too, with its drill sergeant–like demands upon his daily routines. Two bouts with cancer have also bushwhacked Wendell. The death of his wife ransacked his heart and made his bed too empty at night. His hands tremble. His voice sometimes slurs.

Within his motorized chair Wendell does his daily tasks as well as reads his Bible, prays to God, and shares Christ with others out of the praise he finds for God's care of him all these years. To care as a physician of the soul for Wendell, one must account for Wendell's physical body.

In the words of the pastor poet G. M. Hopkins, we are like a "skylark" in our "bone-house," souls and bodies.[1] Early in pastoral leadership, I knew that the battle I fought would not be against "flesh and blood" (Eph. 6:12). But I underestimated how flesh and blood would form the arena for this fight. "Beloved, I pray that all may go well with you and that you may be in good health, as it goes well with your soul" (3 John 2). John the apostle prayed like this, and we learn.

Preparing Our Bodily Senses for Ministry

Let's not forget that we who do the serving are bodily creatures too.

I was asked to visit a middle-aged woman in the community. Mentally, she was four or five, though she had lived forty or fifty years. When I walked through the door, she was bibbed, trying to tackle a plate full of spaghetti. She smiled wide with wonder as I sat down beside her.

"Who are you?" she asked, covered with red sauce and noodle pieces.

"My name is Zack. I am a pastor," I answered.

She immediately and excitedly responded. "I have learned the 'Our Father' by heart," she said. "Wanna hear it?"

"I'd love to," I said.

After proudly reciting the Lord's Prayer, she declared Psalm 23 from memory.

"Did I do good?" she asked.

"You sure did!" I said.

"I believe in God!" she continued. "He loves me. I love him. He died on a cross for me. He will come and take me home one day."

She said this quite seriously, staring straight into my eyes. It was as if she knew what my role was, that to talk about God with a pastor is normal. She was assessing me too. Perhaps detecting what kind of pastor I was. She suddenly dropped her fork, held out her spaghetti-covered, saliva-sprinkled hand, and said, "You wanna pray? Take my hand."

I did, and we prayed to God with our wet spaghetti hands in a living room unknown to the world but cherished by him.

Pause here for a moment. Prayerfully linger with this question: What does it mean for you that ministry is an act of neighbor love and that to love your neighbor will require close physical proximity? If you currently have no patience with the senses, no attentiveness to bodies other than that which is lustful, it is quite possible that you have little idea yet what a pastor's life will actually require of you.

Human Locality

Our pastoral theology in Eden reminds that bodily creatures are local too. They finitely inhabit places.

In the garden that God planted, Adam and Eve ate food, cared for animals, planted seeds, prayed, worked, and loved each other. Theirs was a pornless world with naked rest. Pleasing God meant nothing more than listening to his words, following him in Eden, and gratefully swimming in the safe waters of each other's company. Holding hands, mowing the lawn, resisting foul temptations, and learning to love the one who created them was enough for a significant life with God. But it did not seem to be enough for them. Adam and Eve heard foul whispers slithering in the grass. God's gift of local significance with him began to bore them.

Pause here for a moment. Consider what bores and makes you restless. Consider too what God considers invigorating.

1. We were created to regard God and put nothing else in his place, to surrender to him. In other words, we are to love God.

2. We are to love each other (hold fast to his wife, Gen. 2:24), relate appropriately to our extended family (leave father and

mother, v. 24), and cultivate a community (be fruitful and multiply, Gen. 1:22). In other words, we are meant to love our
neighbors.

3. We are to recognize the goodness and sacredness of the place,
   the creatures, and the things God has created and to watch
   over these good things. We are to contribute to cultivating the
   creation (to work it and keep it, Gen. 2:15) and a culture that
   reflects this given goodness.

These early texts of Genesis teach us that human beings have been
purposed for the love of God and the love of neighbors in a local
place for God's glory. What does this tell us about greatness?

1. God has given you himself to surrender to and love. This means
   that to daily orient your life toward a moment-by-moment relationship with God brings glory to him.

2. God has given you a handful of persons whom you are meant
   to love. You needn't become somebody else or constantly look
   over the shoulders of those people who are right in front of you.
   Attending to God's work among the faces, names, and stories
   where you are is to do already what God considers significant.

3. God will give you a local place to inhabit and a thing to do
   there, which means that you get to become attentive to what is
   there where you are. This means that to dwell knowledgeably
   and hospitably in the place God gives you is to glorify him.

What do you suppose the work of a pastor entails in light of
this? At minimum, we would assume local attentiveness to divine
love, among ordinary people and places, with local weather and
stories. And right here, the words "attentive" to "ordinary people
and local places" challenge our boredom greatly, for we pastors
have a penchant for finding purpose for pastoral work not in Eden
with God, in the grand locality of limits with him, but instead with
the Serpent, who brashly whispered there, speaking illusions of an
unlimited life into the world.

Do You See This Woman, This Man?

"What do you want me to do for you?" Jesus asks.

"Unlimit me and my congregation for God's glory in my generation!" we might say.

But when "unlimit me" becomes our prayer, we are not the first to pray it. A desire like "unlimit me, now!" ruined Eden in the first place and bid Jesus to come and die for us.

I've been asking myself these painful questions. If I am bored with ordinary people in ordinary places, then am I not bored with what God delights in?

If I think that local limits of body and place are too small a thing for a person as gifted as I am, then don't I want to escape what God himself gladly and daily inhabits?

If I stare at a face, a flower, a child, or a congregation and say, "But God, not this. I want to do something great for you!" Am I not profoundly misunderstanding what God says a great thing is?

Pause here for a moment if you can. Linger in these next few sentences.

The woman washed Jesus's feet with her tears and dried them with her hair. The Bible men saw this and grumbled about the "sort" she was. But Jesus withstood their blog-post attacks, their frowns and handshake refusals, their constituency pressures, their threat to discredit him among ministry ranks. As those he trained for ministry watched this scene unfold, Jesus turned his eyes off them, looked instead at her, and asked the leader of these Bible men, "Do you see this woman?" (Luke 7:44).

And what about men? When Luke tells us about the time Jesus called Matthew to follow him, Luke identifies Matthew by his job. Jesus "*saw a tax collector* named Levi, sitting at the tax booth" (Luke 5:27).

But when Mark tells us about that same moment, Mark identifies Matthew not so much by his job but by his pedigree in his family. Jesus "saw *Levi the son of Alphaeus* sitting at the tax booth" (Mark 2:14). I wonder. Did it heal or rust Levi's heart to be

Alphaeus's son in that community? I don't know. What I do know is that when Matthew remembers the moment for himself, he doesn't talk about his family, and he puts his job in the background. "As Jesus passed on from there, *he saw a man* called Matthew sitting at the tax booth" (Matt. 9:9).

The point? Mark saw Matthew's family. Luke saw Matthew's job. Jesus saw Matthew. Suppose you were there in these scenes training for ministry with Jesus.

"Would you see *this* woman?"

"Would you see *this* man?"

One of the lifelong privileges of our pastoral ministry in Jesus is learning to see people as people and ourselves as one of them.

Preaching Barefoot

When a couple enters ministry, the young love of ordinary life can get pressed out of them. She has often just given birth to a child. Or maybe they are newly married. But mostly they are already exhausted from their Bible-training pace, starting the work of ministry as those who already need a break. But to start work for God offers little time for residual fatigue. So the spouse goes with her ministry leader without roots to a new place with a new child and a newer job. The church expects him to hit the ground running. He wants to show that he is worth their hire. He overworks all hours for the sake of Jesus while his new bride and newer baby try to learn to trust Jesus amid the dishwater and *Sesame Street*, with no local friends and no firsthand knowledge of street names. The single person graduating Bible training likewise fills all waking hours for God, exhausts herself, and tells herself that if she ever gets married, then she will slow down (not realizing that the habit of the present pace will be very difficult to interrupt).

Why do we pressure our young ones in ministry to produce ministry results in this way? Why do they feel they must become something other than a normal human being, dwelling physically in a particular place? Why do we imply that in ministry they must become someone other than a young couple in sacred love having their first baby and learning their first call in the world?

My pastor/mentor took his own life amid everything that we all would call success. He had a two-phase building program, was planting churches, and was notable for counsel and conference speaking. But sometimes ministry things that we desire in our culture are not the same as the mattering things Jesus gives us. We tell our businessmen that it is empty to gain the whole world but lose their souls. Is it possible in vocational ministry to do the same?

In my first pastorate we had eighteen acres of land. When I proposed that we cut half of our ministry programs so that our people could rest more with their families and be at home in their neighborhoods with the gospel, some judged me as taking the church backward (even though we had some thirty programs in a church of eighty-five people).

Meanwhile, we could argue tirelessly about our vision statements and eloquently debate tedious questions (such as whether John Calvin would have removed the wooden cross hanging on the wall in our sanctuary, or whether as Protestants we should rebaptize someone previously baptized in the Catholic Church, or whether we should have the name "Presbyterian" in our church logo). But as leaders we often had little ability to show one another the love, grace, or humility of Jesus in our daily relationships. Our dreams and plans for doing something great for God energized us. Our dealings with one another, however, only wounded and fatigued us. It is easy to do a great thing for God so long as greatness does not require interior humility, practical love for the people right in front of us, or submission to the presence of Jesus in the place we already are.

I'm trying to say that when one raging man in Christ becomes gentle, there is more power here than in thirty raging men who came to our ministry event and went home unchanged. But the problem for my heart and for many of those with whom I have served is that thirty in attendance sounds greater than one. And even if, our Lord willing, thirty came and thirty were changed, for all our rejoicing we'd still have to use the bathroom at some point. So mark this down, okay? We too can try to resist our humanity and say an awful thing with conviction in, of all places, a sanctuary while praying, "God, I thank you that I am not like other men" (Luke 18:11). And there it is: the deadly air, the poisoned belief that somehow we who desire to do great things for God don't succumb to being human the way other people do.

Maybe this is why, thirty years after I first spoke my calling in Mrs. Canter's class, I preached barefoot on my first Sunday as a new lead pastor with a second chance. To stand there, holding the Bible on an ordinary and unhidden foundation with my hobbit hairs dangling across my knuckly toes, was an act of personal testimony, a silly but tangible reminder that I am not the Christ.

For too long I had overlooked my being human in my aspirations to greatness. Maybe this is partially what happened to my pastor friend who killed himself. He was a "success." I was becoming one. That's why I said, "Jonathan Edwards farted."

3

Leaving Home

The pastoral ministry is a pilgrimage through the wilderness.

DAVID HANSEN

When a stray dog came onto the property, Papaw would burst through the screen door, scrambling to load his rifle. As the scratched-up metal banged hard against the outside of the house and then slammed back into its place, Papaw, who was by now standing sock-feet and firm on the carport, aimed his gun and fired. He didn't mind the resulting yelp. In fact, he seemed to take pleasure in it as if he had just defended his family from a pack of wolves. He would try to hide a grin and would cuss the yelping mutt like it was a man taunting Papaw to fight. So when my Papaw told me one early Christmas that he was going to shoot Santa Claus, I believed him.

It was not an easy thing to possess a sensitive heart in that dear man's world when he was younger. "Drop your drawers and run, Mamaw! You are a lacy-ruffled pantywaist." That's what Papaw taught me to say to my Mamaw when I was a little boy, and I did. I learned to see women not only by the way Papaw spoke to Mamaw but also by the *Playboy* magazines and the calendars with nudes that were no secret to Mamaw or to us and were strategically placed in the house he built.

At the dinner table, I learned that there was something called "niggers" in the world. Preachers weren't much better in his estimation. The parsonage for the Methodist church was next door. Preachers were nothing but hypocrites, and Papaw had the stories to prove it.

When I came home from elementary school, the first thing Papaw would ask me was if I had received any wuppins from the principal for trouble making that day. When I would answer, "No, Papaw," he would laugh, slap me on the arm, and say, "My lands, boy, what good are you?"

Papaw never sat me down and conducted a class on how to see and interpret stray dogs, women, preachers, or nonwhite skin, but Papaw's way of seeing the world, along with the others in my young life, coached my own.

Ways teach. They form the primary classrooms of our learning. For better and for worse, we learn to see the world and present ourselves in it for witness, not just from creedal statements we learn in class but also from relational mentoring with those with whom we do life (Prov. 13:20; 22:24–25). I am naïve if I believe my current ministry as an adult in St. Louis, Missouri, is a stranger to my Papaw and the ways he and I shared in our common life together in Henryville, Indiana. You are no different.

You and I have learned many things at home, and not all of these things agree with Jesus. What is more, when we leave home for ministry, we take with us, for better and for worse, the things that home taught us.

The Mentoring We Bring with Us

The disciples rebuked children for wanting time with Jesus (Luke 18:15). When a woman broke open an alabaster jar to perfume Jesus with adoration, they gave the woman grief (Matt. 26:7–10). When they saw Jesus talking to a Samaritan, these Jewish disciples

were baffled (John 4:27). Seeing Jesus on the verge of being betrayed, they readied their swords for violence (Luke 22:49). When
they witnessed a rich man walk away from Jesus, they wondered,
"Who can be saved?" (Luke 18:25–26). When the disciples saw a
man born blind, they assumed the disability was punishment for sin
(John 9:1–3). They assumed that differences among Jesus preachers
were cause for immediate dismissal and division (Mark 9:38–41).

The people who lived around the disciples had similar lenses
through which they saw the world. For example, when they saw
Jesus welcome a tax collector, "they all grumbled" (Luke 19:7). A
tomb dweller set into his right mind by Jesus was cause to "leave
their region" (Matt. 8:34). When tragedy struck and innocent people died, folks seriously assumed that tragedy strikes only those
who are worse sinners than others (Luke 13:4).

Each of us carries theologies with a "Big T" and a "little t" into
our ministry. The "Big T" things we learned in class with Bible
teachers. The "little t" theologies we learned, often without knowing it, outside of and regardless of class. Our problem is this: regardless of what we profess about our theology with a "Big T,"
all our little theologies show up at the most unexpected times. For
example, Jesus taught his pastors in training to love their neighbors,
even their enemies. I'm sure that these earnest followers nodded
their heads in agreement with this "Big T." But the first time Samaritans offered offense to Jesus, James and John wanted to kill
them in God's name (Luke 9:54).

Men with Fists and Fears

I was twenty-six in the first year of my first pastorate. The Christian
education meeting had ended but the rage had just begun. This
man, thirty years my senior, started with "Don't you ever . . ." For
the next couple of minutes he let me know that I had no calling
from God and was a disgrace as a pastor, and that as a man I was
only worthy of disrespect. Dipping into the rated-R movie dictionary, he chose words to let me know that if I ever crossed him again

(by which he meant, disagree), I'd be done as a pastor (a threat he later tried to keep). My heart raced. Anxiety flooded my veins. "A soft answer turns away wrath," I remembered (Prov. 15:1). So, I tried, and it didn't. "I'm sorry," I said.

He scowled down closer within head-butting range, raised his tense finger, and threatened, "I'll be watching you to see if you mean it." After a long pause, he burst out of the room. I made my way to my office, fell onto the floor, and cried like a baby (or did I cry like a man?).

How could a man who had sacrificed so much of his resources and time, out of desire for ministry, and who had done so much good, itch for a fight if disagreed with?

How could I crumble like that? The fact is, no matter what I had learned in seminary, when the storm blew out of nowhere and the spit rained down, I may as well have been an eighth grader in the hallway of my stepdad's fists in Clarksville, Indiana.

I was a pastor called by God to do this man and the congregation good by resisting his worst and seeking his best in Christ. But all I saw at the time was a man with fists. Boyhood memories crowded into the room. Boyish fear stole my credentials and hid them in the closet somewhere. I couldn't find them amid the tantrum.

Boyish fear is not the only snapshot of my mentoring history, however. My stepdad boxed me with his open adult hands; the red slap marks across my cheeks and the tears they produced were meant to toughen me. The first time I heard myself as a pastor say, "Do you want to mess with me?" to a man not at his best, in line at a furniture store, I felt surprised and sobered. It caved in on me. I was in danger of proving little different from the men I'd tried to outrun.

As a pastor I see men every day in congregation and community. Some man always sees me too. Jesus sees us both.

Women with Bodies

But men see women too. Hand in hand, my wife and I walk through Llywellyns Pub on a Friday. Men grab her with their eyes. They don't care that I'm hers or that she is mine or that our covenant before God is sacred and happy for us. I've come to learn that she has had to live with the "Do you want to get drunk with me" eyes of men most of her life.

June was known for "putting out." At McDonald's, June was drunk. "Heyyy, Zaacckkk," she called out. "Wanna hang out?" As June winked, slurred, and stumbled, my friends smiled. "Get her in the car," one of them said. "Get her in the car!" I didn't. I wonder where June is now. Has she ever come to know the gracious dignifying rest of the pornless eyes of Jesus? Do I possess such eyes as I open the Bible or pray or eat food in the presence of a woman?

I think of Judy sitting in my church office. "You need to leave him," I said to her about her abusive boyfriend. "I know, but I can't," she said. I prayed silently in my head. I saw the shame in her face. I risked a statement in the context of our history and long knowing. "I'm guessing that the sex isn't even that good," I said gently, almost as a whisper.

She looked at me. Hardened cheeks softened. Then she looked down and the tears began to fall. "No, it isn't," she admitted, shaking her head. "I feel so dirty afterward, the things he wants me to do. I take showers," she said through the tears. "But I can't get clean."

"Then why are you still with him?" I asked. "Because at least for a moment," she says, "at least for a moment, I feel wanted."

I remember my step-grandparents' Playboy Channel, the *Hustler* porn magazines under the sink cabinet in the upstairs bedroom. I think of Papaw's closet. I am crushed with a realization. I cannot see or minister to women until I learn the grace to see through her body to who she is. I write some poetry of my own:

You hid your *Playboys* in the closet
along with everything else.
You hid me there too
and that's what we became.

So, when Jesus asks us, "Do you see this woman?" (Luke 7:44), I wonder what it must have been like for her. There was no lust in his eyes, no use of her behind his smile, no flirtatious familiarity or flattery in his tone. Her given beauty was noticed and cherished; her heart and mind were understood and known. Had she ever been looked at by a man like this? Had the men standing there ever known that they too could learn by grace to look at a woman in this way?

Grandsons can forget that Mamaws are women. Her name was Pauline. His name was Bud. In their youth, I imagine she put on her best dress and touched her neck with perfume, hoping his fingers might gently touch her there too. There was gratitude and tenderness, a longing in his eyes as he spoke her name or recounted her presence. Those years she sat with him in the living room, peeled potatoes with him in the kitchen, lay womanly before him in their bed of years. I like to think that in the end he saw her, and that the years of *Playboys* had their eyes poked out. I like to think that the woman who knew and loved this man of fists found her aging prayers for him answered, as tenderly his fists opened. Fists finally relaxed and caressed, in the bonds of an old promise and a long love.

Race in Conversation

Something else changed too, not fully but truly. Papaw was recovering in Clark County Hospital. He had worked there as a maintenance man for years. Now he was the one needing repair. His heart was tired and wanted to quit early on him. That's why it must have been something for Papaw that day when a stranger came to visit him amid the tubes and monitors that were chained to his arms. That someone was a black chaplain with good news of Jesus, bringing pastoral care for the sick. I wish I could have been a fly on the wall to see that moment.

But as the son of my papaw, I've needed many "black chaplains" myself.

"You are trying too hard," my African American friend said. "You don't have to go to all these racial meetings and planning sessions and events. There's an easier way," he urged. His eyes conveyed his love as he spoke the words. He is old enough to be a father to me.

"What do you mean?" I asked.

"Your office is situated in a little shopping center next door to some black business owners, right? So, how long would it take you to walk from your office to get to one of these businesses?

I paused. I'm sure that I stopped chewing my sandwich too. I could see that a sense of conviction was about to say hello to me. I sat back in the chair. He was smiling now too and gentle.

"About three seconds," I finally answered.

"That's what I'm getting at," he said. "You are trying too hard, speeding around at all these meetings. Instead, walk the three seconds, peek your head in the door, and just say hello. If no one says hello back, try it again next week. If they say hello back, just talk like a human being about human stuff."

I sat there thinking about what he said. I admitted out loud what I was feeling inside.

"Walking the three seconds seems harder. Why is that?" I asked.

He didn't answer. He didn't need to. We both lingered with the thought, eating our french fries.

Jesus enters our mentoring and reshapes the narratives around which we map the world. The disciples grew up hearing stories that implied the poor were in hell and the rich were in heaven. But Jesus inverts this (Luke 16:19–31). Samaritans are noble neighbors (Luke 10:25–37), repenting sinners are justified before God, and arrogant Bible teachers aren't (Luke 18:9–14). And children, far from being merely rebuked and silenced, are what we must become like in order to enter the kingdom of God (Luke 18:15–17). We bring stories of home with us when we enter ministry. Jesus enters them and births new ones for the telling.

The Painful Adjustment

These new narratives of grace for our families don't come cheaply. Not only do we take home with us; we also go back home from time to time. Making this work takes grace and time.

In his own hometown, as long as Jesus was "the carpenter, the son of Mary and brother of James and Joses and Judas and Simon" along with his sisters, Jesus was welcome. He was a member of the people and the place. He grew up there and had a trade like everybody else (Mark 6:3). But once Jesus "began to teach in the synagogue," the welcome mat was removed by most. "They took offense at him" (Mark 6:1–8; Luke 4:16–30).

My way of handling my small resemblance to what Jesus experienced has sometimes made it worse. In trying to separate from what is less like Jesus in our family mentoring, we often do this poorly, like the time I wrote a sixty-page treatise that I called, "Why I'm what some people call 'a Calvinist.'" I made copies and sent them to my family members in Southern Indiana. What better way to show Jesus's love to loved ones than by writing and sending a document they did not expect, to answer questions they were not asking, with a tone that was not warranted, in order to defend an argument that they were not engaged in, and all this by surprise without so much as a conversation?

So when trying to pray or say something of spiritual meaning, family members will not let us forget such things. What a gift of grace this can become. We can all look back and laugh because of the forgiveness needed and given. New family stories can become a source of encouragement to everyone.

But memory of our foolish moments won't let up with other family members. They feel glad for a plumber in the family when the pipes break, or for a hairstylist for free haircuts, but they rarely think of the blessing that a humble minister in the family can provide. They do not recognize the sting we carry with us because of this. Maybe we resemble the hypocrite who hurt them. Their cynicism blames what we represent.

A lot of times, critical voices or implied disappointments come with well-meaning disposition. Our family misses us and wishes we were home. "Son, why have you treated us so?" (Luke 2:48), they might say. Jesus's family felt hurt by Jesus. "Behold," Mary adds, "your father and I have been searching for you in great distress" (Luke 2:48).

Jesus asks a direct and gentle question in response: "Why were you looking for me? Did you not know that I must be in my Father's house?" (Luke 2:49). I wonder what it was like for Joseph to hear that Jesus had to be in the house of a different Father, and that this Father was not Joseph and did not include Joseph's provision or dwelling. That must have hurt.

As Jesus and his family began this painful adjustment, his family "did not understand" what Jesus was trying to reveal to them (Luke 2:50). They would have to ponder these things in their hearts and chew on it all for a while (Luke 2:51).

A Time to Stand

So by the time the crowds gather and Jesus has had no time to eat, his family responds poorly. They could have brought food to encourage him that the Lord, who called him, would sustain him and be faithful to him. But instead they looked right into the good that Jesus did and disparaged his character. While others gather to learn from God through Jesus, "his mother and his brothers" stand outside (Mark 3:31). In that public moment they refer to him as a man not in his right mind (Mark 3:21). Humanly speaking, there are very few critiques more painful than those leveled at us by those who have known us longest.

Normally, Jesus marveled at this unwelcome at home, endured the pain of it, and simply continued on with his ministry (Mark 6:5–6). But the time had come. From the age of twelve Jesus had submitted and respectfully loved his family, even while they did not understand him. But now at thirty, he will fulfill his calling, whether they understand it or not. There are things that even they must learn from God. They cannot continue to pick at him like this. The manipulation, the name-calling, and the use of guilt to shame has to stop. Jesus will love them, but he will no longer indulge their mischaracterizations of him or their interpretations about who God is and how God's ministry is supposed to work. The family and Jesus must surrender to God's purposes for them and not the other way around. Jesus will go on in his calling now, whether they want him to or not, whether they are embarrassed by him or not, whether they don't think he treats them well enough or not. "Who are my mother and my brothers?" (Mark 3:31–35) he says. This moment in Jesus's life floors me.

The family must have gone home that day furious or pained. Jesus only confirmed their suspicions. He is out of his mind. They are right to stand outside and not join in. Or maybe they genuinely believed that he cared more about others than he cared about them. Maybe they felt disrespected because he spoke so plainly. Maybe they thought what a selfish and proud man their son and brother was, who loved the crowds and the fame and the attention.

What we know for sure is that while Jesus gave himself to the Father's business, Jesus did not stop loving his family (John 19:26). In time, his mother would come to understand all those things that had been prophesied and treasured within her heart. In time his brother James would affectionately bow to him as Lord and Savior. But we do not see them all together very much.

Extended-family perceptions, hometowns, and ministries are a mess—it was this way even for our Lord in the fullness of his humanity. But even here, grace doesn't quit.

Conclusion

I was leaving the Guernseys' Thanksgiving gathering. It had been thirty-five years or so since Papaw told me he planned to shoot Santa; six or seven years since the arrival of the black chaplain; and six or seven years since I had written a letter telling him of my love for him and of Jesus, that letter that he called "a keeper." It was a year or two prior to Mamaw's death. It was after fifty years of Mamaw's praying.

"What do you know, young man?" he said, silver-haired and thin. Long gone were the once strong sideburns, dark and full on his now sunken cheeks. The seriousness and clarity in his brown eyes surprised me. "Not many people know what's inside this old man."

"Yah?" I asked.

"Two years ago, this old man began to give thanks to God every night," he said. "A few months ago, this old man started going back to church."

I was stunned with the sacredness of this moment. I foraged through my keys toward the empty deep of my jeans pockets trying to find words. "What is that like for you, Papaw?" I mustered.

"Well, I don't go along with all of it," he said. "But to tell you the truth, I've missed it."

He stepped toward me to hug me.

Then he smiled as he spoke. "You never know what will happen to this old man, do you?"

"You never know."

4

Invisible

The fact is pastors are invisible six days a week. . . . A great deal of our most important work is done behind the scenes.

EUGENE H. PETERSON

What we've said so far:

Pastors crave.

Pastors preach with skin and bone.

Our hurry doesn't help much.

Bored with true greatnesses given, we try to leave home but take it with us.

Worn out with false greatnesses chased.

Drenched with successes but dry with God.

Asking old questions, new, this looking back.

What is a pastor for anyway?

Humdrum Work

"I want to thank you for what you said the last time we met."

He said this in a coffee shop. My friend's small child would say with toddler speech, "I don't wike God" or "I don't pray." Pained, these parents worried they were doing something wrong.

In response, I said something about how a lot of us as adults don't like God in our lives or don't want to pray.

"Maybe the god your child doesn't like is a god we wouldn't like or believe in either; not a true picture of God as he is at all," I suggested. Then I paused. I wasn't sure as usual that what I was prayerfully trying to grasp was on target. I was praying in that strange way that we quietly can, in between sentences, among those small silences that linger as we dig our spoon into a bowl of hot broth.

"Instead of trying to get your young one to stop speaking her dislike for God," I said, "what would it be like to admit our sometimes dislike for God even as adults and let this form your prayers together? After all, the Psalms or Ecclesiastes, Jonah or Job show us such prayers. They teach us that God listens to us in Christ even when we have feelings that are ugly and even when such ugly feelings are directed his way. What if right now this is what your toddler gets to learn with you? And maybe instead of reading the Bible for a season, you invite your kids to act out the scenes written there in the Gospels? Someone gets to be the person who is sick. Another gets to be the Pharisee who is mad. And someone gets to say what Jesus did and reach out to the sick one, right there in your living room."

In the weeks following those words, something wonderful happened. Their child began to relate to prayer differently, and spoken dislike for God faded. A moment like this helps us understand why it is not easy to describe what a pastor does. It also puts boredom and our restless desire for larger, more famous legacies into spotlight.

- *Mundane.* This moment is barely noticeable in the world and will have no record in history. Two men ate soup and talked for a few minutes on a Tuesday in a Missouri town.

- *Invisible.* No one else in the congregation saw it or knows about it.

- *Uncontrollable.* There is no formula. I'd never been asked that question before and could just as easily have not known what to say or missed the mark completely. Prayers were spoken. Stepping forward was an act of waiting on God in the unknown.

- *Unfinished.* We said grace and gave thanks with laughter at the telling of this good news. But we both know that this toddler has a whole lifetime ahead in which to make her life what it will be with God or otherwise. "Ten years from now," I say, "maybe we'll be sitting here in this same old shop, eating soup, talking about your toddler who by then will be a teenager! We'll be looking together to the Lord again for sure, seeking all the help and grace we can get!" We laugh and shake our heads.

We walk out into the parking lot. With no more words to say, we pat each other's back the way men often do. He goes back to his office. I head on to meet with another.

I didn't envision this kind of daily life. I thought of a pastor as something akin to an itinerant conference speaker, prophetically originating and preaching vision for large crowds and organizations, so that I can constantly demonstrate that we are not like other churches and I am not like other preachers. Weekly, I would mobilize and manage programs, hiring, firing, and training personnel, so that by the force of my personality, the expertise of my organizational leadership, and the savvy uniqueness of our brand presence, I (I mean we, of course) can build a more notable gospel platform from which I (uh, I mean, we) can rise into greater gospel prominence, and then I (I don't mean we) can leave and move on to bigger and better gospel things for God.

But if I aspire to this other vision, who will sit without haste listening for God over soup in the middle of an ordinary day in a mundane place so that an unknown-to-the-world family who loves Jesus can find their way in him in the midst of what actually hurts them, confuses them, or thrills them most?

The Fame-Shyness of Jesus

Yet I crave words like these, which were spoken to Jesus: "Everyone is looking for you" (Mark 1:37).

These are fame words. And yet if Jesus was the famous one, why would people need to *look for him*? Conventional wisdom would agree with the counsel of Jesus's own family. "No one works in secret if he seeks to be known openly. . . . Show yourself to the world," they cynically urged (John 7:4). They did not understand why a great worker for God would choose a manner of life that could be characterized by working "in secret." I'm not sure that I, or most of the church communities I have served, have understood this either. So public was the buzz about Jesus that he could not openly enter a town (Mark 1:45). Shouldn't he seize this platform for God?

And yet his brothers recognized something about Jesus that irritated them. As I begin to see it, it irritates me too (in the sense of conviction). Jesus is fame-shy. Jesus seemed drawn not to the spotlight but from it. Disciples and friends had to search. He wasn't tweeting. His blog lay unattended. His e-mail responses were not immediate. Where they often found him was alone and in desolate places praying (Luke 5:16). In fact, it seems that just when Jesus was at the right place at the right time, and the opportunity to advance his work through greater celebrity called out to him, he intentionally allowed the call to go to voice mail and disappeared for a while (John 6:15).

Jesus would have driven any publicist and congregation mad. In fact, after he did something great, Jesus often asked that no one say anything about it.[1] Perhaps Jesus's asking no one to speak was partly a marketing ploy of false humility. Entertainers do this when, with one hand, they indicate that they do not want our applause, while, with the other hand, they simultaneously encourage it. Or maybe it would have simply proved impractical for Jesus to freely minister to others if everyone had known who he was. We see this analogy with rock stars and celebrities of our own day who have to travel at odd times or wear disguises when in public.

But as I revisit these explanations, what if Jesus's reason for quieting the talk about himself was actually born out of living what he taught? "Beware of practicing your righteousness before other people in order to be seen by them," he said (Matt. 6:1).

We can somehow diminish God-glorifying things when we "sound [the] trumpet" so that all can see us (Matt. 6:2). He believed that doing great things for God is done best with our left hand not knowing what our right hand is doing—when our practices for him go unnoticed and unacknowledged by the press, the church, and even those closest to us (Matt. 6:3). Questions pester me: Do I possess a stamina for going unnoticed? Can I handle being over-looked? Do I have a spirituality that equips me to do an unknown thing for God's glory?

No wonder Paul waited years before he told a soul about an experience he'd had with God. He wouldn't even tell it as his own. He told it like it was someone else's story, to deflect attention from himself (2 Cor. 12:2–4).

Jesus doesn't deny the tempting benefits of fame. We gain real reward from another's applause. But when the applause dies, so does its provision (Matt. 6:5). The shining moment fades into the empty theater of our lives where the fundamental questions still remain. So three times, as Jesus catalogs the righteous things we do, he compels us to consider "your Father who sees in secret" (Matt. 6:4; see also vv. 6, 18). In so doing, he recovers a sense of Eden. We were meant to live beneath the gaze of our Creator freed from seeking fame from others.

A troubling thought comes to my mind. How does the fame indifference of Jesus inform the way we go about growing our ministries or fashioning a ministry for him? Are we willing to forgo what works in the world for what Jesus teaches us to trust? I'm confounded.

An empowering thought resurfaces. God is the remembered one. But this does not mean we are forgotten—not by him. Not by a long shot. In fact, being remembered by him means we no longer fear being forgotten by the world. Living humanly within his remembrance is enough.

Invisible People, Invisible Prayers

Jesus powerfully lives out this gem of a truth and purchases it for us. Have you ever noticed the Jesus way of strategic networking in Luke's Gospel? It is almost nonexistent (at least, as it relates to being in the know and connecting with those who matter). Jesus seems intent on noticing and orienting his schedule around the unnamed mountains in his range. He makes personal visits to the physically and spiritually ill that include a mother-in-law, a leper, a paralytic, and a tax collector (Luke 4–5). Then there was the man with the withered hand, the sickness of a Gentile's servant, and a widow and her dead son (Luke 6–7).

Jesus finally spends time with hundreds in a crowd. But within that crowd it is not the well known, the rich, or the connected that Jesus seeks out. The sick and the troubled remain his focus (Luke 6:17–18).

Even John the Baptist is confused. Jesus's way of doing a day seems strategically off. "Are you the one who is to come, or shall we look for another?" John asks (Luke 7:19). Isn't it strange that a life of loving unknown people in their miseries should cause others of us to wonder if it is time to move on from Jesus?

But assuring John through the Scriptures that this way of spending time is exactly what God would have Jesus do, Jesus met with a sinful woman and then with several ordinary and broken women. And then miles away there was a man who howled naked in the tombs among the Gentiles (Luke 7–8). Jesus sought him out too.

At this point, some crowds become confused about Jesus's behavior. They ask Jesus to leave them alone (Luke 8:34). Jesus grants their request. He is willing to let a crowd gather without him. He then spends time with another sick woman and the sick daughter of a synagogue ruler (Luke 8:40–56).

Herod the king now becomes perplexed and desires an audience with Jesus. Jesus seems to have no interest in changing his schedule to make such an appointment (Luke 9:7–9)! Instead, Jesus sends his disciples to spend time with those who are physically and mentally troubled. Then he begins to talk about dying and a cross that must in time become both his and theirs (Luke 9:21–27).

Finally, Jesus reveals himself as the very Son of God, greater than Moses and Elijah! But he limits this view to only three people, and no one is to speak of it (Luke 9:29–36).

In fact, throughout this time Jesus continues to withdraw to desolate places for extended times of prayer (Luke 4:42; 5:16; 6:12; 11:1). After spending time with some Samaritans and two obscure women who were friends of his (Mary and Martha), the disciples (who were recently wondering which of them would become the most famous, Luke 10:46–48) finally notice Jesus's way of life, and they say to him, "Lord, teach us to pray" (Luke 11:1).

At long last, Jesus begins to engage the well-connected and influential persons of his community. But these conversations are anything but diplomatic. They end with a highly respected lawyer saying to Jesus, "Teacher, in saying these things you insult us" (Luke 11:45). And as for the elite leaders in the community? Their response to all this is to lie "in wait for him, to catch him in something he might say" (Luke 11:54).

Jesus's idea of doing great things for God meant a daily routine that accentuated a greatness of a different kind. His schedule among the least looked something like what follows.
In particular:

Early morning and late evening: disappear often and pray.

After breakfast till just before dinner: seek out unknown and scarily broken people and give them the bulk of your time. Set aside times to teach publicly and to debrief privately with those you are mentoring.

Early evening after dinner: spend time together and enjoy each other.

In general:

Eat and sleep.

Help those other leaders who are for you to understand from God's Word that this way of ministry is from God and is no waste.

Bear with people whom you help but who distance themselves from you because your way of life and ministry scares them.

Don't worry that your true glory is veiled to almost everyone around you.

Don't schedule too much time with those who believe themselves to be pillars in the government or the church. Remember that they too are just people. They have their own sins to repent of and their own callings to fulfill. They are not more important than the broken and the lost for whom you're called.

Attending the Jesus Seminary

Withdrawal to prayer? Prioritized time with ordinary and broken people unnoticed by the world? An active indifference to those who do have clout? Jesus's way is not the celebrity way.

Perhaps this is why Jesus trained laborers for ministry so differently from us. Notice, for example, where Jesus leads his disciples to make them fishers of men (Mark 1:17–45). He takes them out among the sick, the poor, the demon possessed, and people from everywhere around, which included teachers, urban hipsters, rural folks, and Peter's mother-in-law. At one point the disciples are surrounded by all the sick and demon possessed from the area. Imagine what it would have meant to follow and learn from Jesus in the midst of these tragic and putrid sights, sounds, and smells.

Throughout the Gospels we consistently observe Jesus teaching theology in the midst of the psych ward. He sat his apprentices down in the emergency room, as it were. He introduced them to ghastly sights, grieved sounds, and rank aromas of actual human people in their diseases, their wrestling with demons, their disputes, their poverty, and their loss of spouses. He brought them near to ethnic prejudices, injustices, anxieties, and traumas, not to mention the joys, pleasures, delights, and longings of ordinary human beings. Jesus's disciples learned about God in the context of the bodily life situations that actually exist in the world, the sensory ramifications of an under-the-sun reality.

Imagine learning our doctrine of God by studying our best theologians while sitting in the ER amid anxious parents, traumatized children, gunshot wounds, and asthma attacks. Imagine reading theology amid the stale smell of coffee, the sound of tears, and the sights of perplexity, trauma, and frustration. How would this impact how we process the doctrines and categories of God's omnipotence, omnipresence, and omniscience? Or what if we read our doctrine of salvation where mental patients spook the halls, where medications, prayers, and helpless parents wrestle with insurance, paperwork, and the pressure of strained budgets?

Within such daily bodily rhythms, no wonder Jesus withdrew at strategic times for prayer and invites us to follow him.

But This Doesn't Work!

I spoke with a pastor who serves a large, famous, and praised congregation. But internally and privately, the pastoral staff is worn out and hurting. He explained, "Over the last several weeks I've been working with our staff to identify the currently practiced values of our church—not the values we hope our church has but the values revealed in the complaints, the ways, and the desires expressed among those who attend."

He paused, looked down, and shook his head.

"We determined that our church culture values professionalism, excellence, and the Bible. Professionalism is interpreted in such a way that transparency or relational honesty is suspect and a sign of weakness. Excellence means that it is hard to be human. Any mistake is quickly or harshly criticized. Our stance on the Bible, as interpreted through this view of professionalism and excellence, means that Bible information is prized, but not if it exposes or melts us, and not if it is taught without the highest academic standards. "

He continued: "We tried recently to invite church members for dinner with no agenda other than to get to know one another. Many told us afterward that, as pastors, we had wasted their time because we gave them nothing to do but sit with people, talk, eat, and watch children play."

As I listened, my heart was pained. This dear pastor was worn out with the years of constant pressure to veil his heart, to make no mistakes, and to have constant and new information from the Bible to pass on. In this environment in which cultivating relationships is viewed as a waste of time, I said something about a quote from Eugene Peterson's book *Under the Unpredictable Plant*.[2]

"Yeah, I don't read Eugene Peterson anymore," he said with a pained smile. "He draws out my longings for what a community of Jesus followers is supposed to be and how my time as a pastor is meant to be spent. But then I face my actual day in this system, and I cannot get from here to there and still keep my job. Our Lord knows I've tried."

Then he said something insightful: "In order for this church to grow in health, it will require a culture change. But that would mean we'd probably lose several hundred people. As soon as we imply that the gospel shows strength in weakness, grace for our mistake making, and biblical truth as having a relational context and a sacramental view of time, many will be agitated and leave. The good news is that we'd no longer bow to immature and damaging congregational assumptions and would finally try to pastor them into more of a Jesus way," he said.

Then he smiled with irony. "But here is the rub: even though those who stayed would join us in trying to replace our celebrity mind-set with a Jesus one, our external community as a whole would observe this loss of people at our established church and conclude that we as pastors had failed. We'd be known in the surrounding community and denomination as the ones on whose watch the church went from two thousand to fifteen hundred members or less. Because of that, I don't think our leaders have much of a stomach for this redirection. We are stuck, and so am I."

No simplistic answer exists here. A counter church culture that is "organic," "edgy," and "casual" can just as easily become celebrity measures by which we compare ourselves, judge others, and keep our followings. Maybe you've noticed this too. Those brothers and sisters who struggle with Jesus's challenge to the celebrity of professionalism and excellence generally dress alike: business formal or business casual. Those brothers and sisters who struggle with Jesus's challenge to the celebrity of organic and edgy likewise generally dress alike: slim jeans, obscure T-shirt, large watch band, thin-rimmed glasses. In both cases, we have to acknowledge the elephant in the room—we give large amounts of detailed attention to how we appear.

Trusting Jesus More Than Appearances

Where does all this lead us? The pastor has two fears, and so do most of us: (1) people will leave; (2) we will be judged as failures. These two mantras—keep people coming and keep up our approval rating—are the celebrity way.

Consequently, it is no easy task to say, "Enough of this!"

Courage is required, because some will put our jobs on the line if we seek to make these kinds of changes to the celebrity mind-set (John 12:42). We will actually get passed over and reduced in influence should we persist.

Patience is demanded, because Jesus's categories for success are so foreign to so many of us—this kind of change does not happen overnight.

Grace is necessary, because who could risk such loss in our ecclesiastical and cultural worlds, and who could love long and steadily enough for change apart from him?

At this point, we need two reminders set before us.

First, people criticized, resisted, overlooked, and left Jesus. Remember, Jesus had a death threat over his life because he healed someone. Crowds of thousands were reduced to twelve because Jesus exposed their misguided reasons for following him (John 6:1–15). Think about that for a while. Doing what will mend others in the gospel will rile and outrage some. Size of crowd has nothing to do with it.

Second, if a crowd reduces because the manner, ways, and values of Jesus are absent in a leader, then change is rightly called for. But if crowds leave because the actual manner and value system of Jesus have confronted and confounded the allure of a world/flesh/Devil mind-set, then it is time to support that leader. He needs our help, not our harm. He has enough of that already.

Already Discovered

I was a long-haired college kid. Bob was a campus minister with the Navigators Christian ministry. He regularly invited me to come with him for prayer in forgotten places. I look back now and marvel that Bob saw this as no waste of time. I'm grateful. Often, after a couple of prayerful hours, we would sit together to talk. One time, Bob looked at me.

"Zachary," he said. "You are already discovered."

"What?" I asked.

"Whatever happens in your future, with all you dream and hope for, I want you to know that getting discovered has already happened to you. Jesus already knows you, hears your prayers, and delights to know you."

I think back to those words. Was I already discovered by Jesus long before seminary, internships, awards, travels, books, and sadly mistaken ten-year projections? Already known before the rubble and the ruin, preaching barefoot in the sanctuary of second chances?

How could this be, unless Jesus made a habit of giving his time to unknown, broken people in out-of-the-way places, overlooked by the world, but delighted in by him?

The thought occurs to me. It stops me in my tracks. If Jesus's pastoral work consisted of doing large things famously as fast as he could in the most efficient way possible, I would never have known him.

PART TWO

The Temptations
We Face

5

Everywhere for All

There is a day, when the road neither comes nor goes, and the way is not a way but a place.

WENDELL BERRY

It's as obvious as air.

In order to do something, you have to be somewhere.

Yet there's more.

Eventually, you get to where you're going. Have you thought of that?

It's one thing to do what you need to in order to get somewhere.

It's quite another to know how to stay put for a while once you've gotten there.

Searching for Roots

"Zack, your life is like a five-alarm fire. You are coming and going in so many directions. I worry about you." Bill's words shook me as a young man.

One of my bosses echoed the same sentiment ten years later. "You are doing so many different things," she said. "We want you around here for a long time, so pace yourself, okay?"

Two colleagues invited me to lunch. Another called on the phone. "We are worried about you," they all said.

Then I received a letter. It was the old-fashioned kind with a stamp on the envelope. I opened it and heard my mom's voice as I read. She too must have heard the alarm. "Son," she wrote, "a tree has to have roots to provide shade."

Mark this down, okay? You and I were never meant to repent for not being everywhere for everybody and all at once. You and I are meant to repent because we've tried to be.

Advancing by Limitation

A young woman wrote down everything she would not have if she chose for her life a poet's vocation. She took stock of her truer loves and forsook all other possible and imagined lives for the sake of a poet's life.[1]

When I became a pastor I made no such list. I never imagined that if I said, "Jesus, take me anywhere and everywhere with you!" that I might have to watch him say yes to others who brought the same request but hear him say no to me instead (Mark 5:19).

It's not because the Bible didn't prepare me for this. The apostle Paul put a list like the poet's in broad daylight for all to see. But I was too busy studying 1 Corinthians 12 or Romans 12 for exams that required my views on tongues, prophecy, apostles, and miracles. I never actually reckoned with the plain and simple message of Paul's words—mainly, that some people have this gift but not that one, and these boundaries reveal God's provision for our good. Paul says that the hand needs the foot, and the eye needs the ear. I would have resisted, supposing that I could become all four!

And never would I have imagined that the calling given to me out of Christ's love might be considered "weaker," "less honorable," or "unpresentable" in comparison to others' (1 Cor. 12:22–26).

On the contrary, when I read in Jesus's story that God gives some of us five talents, some of us two, and some of us one, naturally I assumed that I had five (Matt. 25:14–30). When I read Jesus's story about some who produced a crop, one hundred, sixty, or thirty times what was sown, I never imagined that I might be the guy with thirty, living my life in the shadows of my colleagues who produce one hundred (Matt. 13:18–23).

My point is this. If we want to use our gifts, we are required to take a step. But in whatever direction we place our foot, we necessarily leave every other direction empty for the footsteps of another.

So if Jesus had asked me, "What would you like me to do for you?" I would never have responded, "Lord, I desire a vocation that limits me and makes me dependent upon others." But it's plain that I'm meant to. "And he gave the apostles, the prophets, the evangelists, the shepherds and teachers . . . ," Paul says (Eph. 4:11). As a pastor, I may be apostolic, but I'm not an apostle. I'm prophetic, perhaps, but not a prophet. I'm evangelistic but not an evangelist. My vocation, therefore, is not itinerant and mobile like these other three.

I am, in contrast, a pastor teacher. Pastor means "shepherd." Shepherds are the returning ones. Shepherds remain when the apostle, the prophet, and the evangelist arrive and then move on. Heart-oriented questions confront us here. What will it mean to our lives to have a vocation of learning how to return? What will it mean to let go of an itinerant life?

Learning how to stay put gives me fits. Rarely in my life have I known people who stay with one another, in families or churches or denominations. How can a broken-homed, upwardly mobile, restless-for-something-larger, more notable-and-now kind of man ever become a pastor?

Jesus.

Learning the Names of Trees

I grew up in the Ohio River Valley, in the lower southeast region of Indiana near Louisville, Kentucky. Many of those towns are named after men—Charlestown, Georgetown, Scottsburg. In Clarksville I learned confidence with football and shyness with girls. In Floyd's

Knobs I learned to drive. As a teenager I could drive Buck Creek Road with my eyes closed.

But Henryville is designated as the glue for my life. My name is scribbled in chalk there in a closet underneath the stairs in the house that my papaw built. The Henryville United Methodist Church has had a long, beautiful, and sometimes tumultuous relationship with my family. Mount Zion Cemetery gives rest to many of my people— those I have known, loved, and miss—and those I've only heard stories about. In fact, my mom and my pop, the Guernseys and the Eswines, both have their roots in this small town. My papaw had a mug down at Tanners reserved just for him. He and his long-time friends had named themselves "the liars' club." They sat most mornings to enjoy each other's company before the work of the day began. There are people who live in Henryville who once changed my diaper. I meet them at funerals. Just by looking at me, they tell me that I must be Vern's son.

It was the demons that first drew my attention to Jesus's sense of place (I refer, of course, to those demons that the Bible mentions). I'm not accustomed to learning from demons. A man who has little time for the trees on his property will have even less time for unseen spooks. But Mark's Gospel records a conversation between Jesus and demons. "What have you to do with us, Jesus of Nazareth?" they hissed. "Have you come to destroy us? I know who you are— the Holy One of God" (Mark 1:24).

The demons first identified Jesus with Nazareth; and, second, they knew this Jesus as the Holy One from God. I pondered the con-nection. I rolled it over in my mind. Jesus *of Nazareth* is *the Holy One of God*. The Holy One of God is Jesus *of Nazareth*. Suddenly the nightlight was turned on. I saw in the room what had before eluded me. If the Holy One of God is Jesus *of Nazareth*, then the Holy One of God has a hometown.[2] The shade giver has roots.

Jesus was at one place, not every place in the world. He had a home church. He had a family and a trade that was known and sometimes challenged by his community (Luke 4:16–30). If the

Ohio River looms ever present in my upbringing, for Jesus it was the River Jordan. I fished and boated in Patoka and Deam Lakes. The lake known as the Sea of Galilee offered shores, waters, and fish for Jesus. He knew the shortcuts and paths in the Galilee region as I knew those particular to the Ohio Valley. The Holy One of God became a man—and this incarnation included limiting himself and inhabiting a locality on the earth.

And while in this place, Jesus knew the names of trees. He built from them what his mind imagined and what his skill learned over time could call forth. Amid the aromas of freshly cut woods, the bone and blood in Jesus's hands would form an alliance. He would shape and sand long trunks and planks of wood into tables and chairs.

Jesus crafted these barks during what theologians refer to as his "years of obscurity." I think of this when I remember my Papaw and Mamaw visiting my home in St. Louis. They told me in a few minutes what I had not learned in two years—the names of the trees and bushes on my rented property. We walked slowly. I needed to listen, but listening required resting. I struggled with both as Papaw and Mamaw named my place for me.

I'm trying to say how restless this all makes me! I'm puzzled over what Jesus is doing among the wood chips. Aren't you? What is the meaning of this sawdust caught in Jesus's beard and dangling from his smile—and all this tree-bark obscurity for thirty years? Thirty years! Jesus had a world to save, injustice to confront, lepers to touch. Isn't greatness for God squandered by years of obscurity? What business does a savior have learning the names of trees?

Climbing Mountains

In my white-collar pastor world, we plan in order to meet, and we meet in order to plan. "Somewhere else doing something else" is the unspoken motto of our missional advancement. Bigger means holier and better. As one lead pastor said, explaining why he rarely spent time with his staff, "We will have all kinds of time to meet together in heaven. But now we have work to do! We have souls to save and disciples to make."

This idea seems so foreign to the carpenter in Nazareth. In places like Nazareth or Henryville, advancement to somewhere else doing something else is rare. In contrast to white-collar pastors and people, blue-collar churches learn to testify about what they've seen and heard in the ordinary of the day, because the ordinary of the day is the great thing that happened. What one lived that day becomes what one actually talks about that night.

For example, the granddaughter's smile down at the A&P becomes a fifteen-minute story that draws everyone into belly laughter. The smile was important enough to notice and the story valuable enough to tell. The laughter, the story, and the smile each form a sufficient agenda for conversation. Nothing more is required to share time together. In my younger years, I found this attention to the mundane lacking. As I became certain of my pastoral vocation, I wanted "real" conversation about "real" life. I wanted us to talk about things that mattered, things that make a difference. Now I'm beginning to reflect more on those feelings. When did it happen that to talk about what one lives is not enough for real conversation? When did it happen that a granddaughter's smile is not substantial enough to speak of, especially for a pastor given to bear witness to God in a locality?

When George Mallory was once asked why he wanted to climb Mount Everest, he famously answered, "Because it is there." But in a personal letter to George's wife, Ruth, he revealed even more about what drove him to climb the mountain. "Dearest," he wrote, ". . . you must know that the spur to do my best is you and you again. . . . I want more than anything to prove worthy of you." George left a meaningful legacy that proved worthy of history's remembrance. But George's son John wrote something that has challenged me. Proud of his father but sad too, John wrote, "I would so much rather have known my father than to have grown up in the shadow of a legend, a hero, as some people perceive him to be."[3]

The answers George gave concerning his motives have confronted my own. The mountain "was there," but so was John, George's son. The mountain brought a sense of joy and gave a sense of the human struggle upward for life itself. But George's knowing his son would have brought him joy and a sense of striving for the purpose of life too. Climbing the mountain enabled George to prove worthy of his family. But so would have loving and providing for his family in the ordinary routines of a long life, day upon day. So why did George choose to engage the challenges of the mountain but not the living room?

At this point, I am leery, sensing that I have established a false dichotomy between one's work or dreams and one's family and routine. After all, there is nothing morally wrong with climbing Mount Everest. George Mallory was a schoolmaster with three children. Though he and Ruth were geographically apart as much as they were together, there is indication that this was not easy on George. So I must refocus the question. Why did George Mallory choose the mountain when he understood that it might take his life?[4] Why was Mallory's pursuit of joy, the meaning of life, the worthiness of family, and the loyalty to complete a task connected more with climbing a mountain than with the daily routines of love and life, work and play in community at home?

I think of my Lord learning the names of trees in Nazareth.

I hear the Serpent's whisper.

What if, for many of us, the ordinary is the larger mountain?

Learning How to Return

It feels strange to say it. But the Christmas shepherds are providing me texts for pastoral theology. They are skilled in dealing with anticlimax. Remember?

Angels infiltrate the skies right before the shepherds' eyes. The glory of God thunders in chorus. Ancient promises are fulfilled and witnessed. Fear seizes these sheep men. Good tidings are spoken to them. "The Savior is born, and this will be the sign that will confirm it for you." To see and hear angels was spectacular already. Imagine how spectacular the Messiah's sign could be. Perhaps God would reach down his hand and create a new planet. Then he could hold it between his thumb and index finger and place the planet in its new position in the universe right before their very eyes! Surely this would be a sign worthy of a savior from God!

But here the anticlimax begins. No planets were formed. "You will find a baby," they said, "wrapped in swaddling cloths and lying in a manger." The sign of God's fame lay in the aroma of cattle and hay—the placenta of new birth, the cries and warmth of ordinary life.

> No stately form that we should know him
> There was no halo on his head
> No trumpets blowing
> No majestic fanfare
> He was born where animals are fed.

To these ordinary sheepherders, God has revealed glorious and fantastic wonders! And now, the second anticlimax confronts us. According to the Gospel of Luke, after beholding and participating in this too-grand-for-words event, "the shepherds returned" (Luke 2:20). They returned? This fact confounds me. After beholding the glory, the shepherds went home.

Same Old, Same Old

How could this happen? They were shepherds, men who worked with their hands. The aroma of animal and outdoor living took up residence in their skin. These were blue-collar workers, salt-of-the-earth kinds of folks. They understood what it meant to work the late shift. "By night," Luke says, they watched their flocks (Luke 2:8). *Watching*, make no mistake, is an adrenaline word. Shepherding meant keeping their eyes open when most in their community were closed. Years of this kind of labor creates a complaint in one's joints and bones. Add to this the scorn and jokes that were leveled against the shepherding way of life, and my restless question seems all the more valid. Why didn't the shepherds go on the road?

With all that they had seen, they could have started a conference series, planned a book tour, and instantly gained thousands of blog followers. Doing the same thing in the same place for the rest of their lives was their lot and their legacy. They could have changed all that. The celebrity moment had found them. Greatness is too worthy a thing to demean by returning to the ordinary of life!

But right here, God in his grace disrupts us. By means of the shepherds returning, God seems to seriously imply that seeing God's glory, hearing his voice, receiving his good news, and beholding his love was never meant to deliver us from ordinary life and love in a place—it was meant instead to provide the means to preserve us there.

Pause here. Don't rush past what I just said.

Celebrity opportunity does not remove the arrangements for neighbor love that still exist. Someone will still need to care for the sheep, create clothes for others, provide milk and food for neighbors. And even if the shepherds did get on a tour bus and travel around together, their call to love each other and their neighbors, to eat, to wash clothes, to seek and give forgiveness from each other in ordinary moments, to attend to sickness, to celebrate birthdays, and to seek God would not go away.

Every addict knows this. The glorious moment provided by the drug does not remove the ordinary call of life. That is the problem. The high doesn't last. We crash, and our loved ones are still there, longing to do ordinary life together and pained that it is being taken from them.

Every hero knows this. The man who kicks the goal that wins the World Cup knows that tomorrow night or next season he has to start again—another game is coming. He also still has to learn how to listen to his wife and cherish her, to resist exasperating his kids, to learn how to give his heart authentically to God and to receive God's love and wisdom for his life. The fireman who saves the life, the CEO who saves the day financially, the mother who saves the day for a child—the heaven-like moment thrills and celebrates. But it isn't heaven.

For the shepherds "to return" expresses the wisdom of God. We return to the same old, same old, but we are changed and empowered to dwell there relishing what we've witnessed of his grace.

But someone will say, "That's a nice sentiment, but social media allows me to be everywhere at once. Pastors are no longer limited."

All I can tell you is that my book had won an award. Those who heard my radio interview were greatly helped and let me know it. But I gave that interview red-eyed and in my pajamas from a retreat house in the woods of Missouri. I was broken down. I could never have spoken in person that way, and if I had tried, I would have had to do a great deal of pretending. My point is that no matter how far technology allows our gifts to travel, we ourselves, the persons that we actually are, remain rooted to one place at one time.

I tweet you, with my particular rump seated on this particular chair, on this old and slow laptop in this room. I am not everywhere at once. I am only here—one place at a time. In the fullness of Jesus's humanity, so was he. In order to follow Jesus we have to go through a carpenter's shop in Nazareth.

Going Somewhere by Staying Put

Several times I've spoken with pastors who crave to leave their present place and calling, not rightly, because of burnout or safety for themselves or their family, but because of the limits and boredom or hard work they feel amid the rough terrain of the same old, same old. Remaining put while other colleagues seem to advance and move up to more exciting and seemingly influential ministry callings, amid a culture that praises them and overlooks us, only intensifies the restlessness. So these pastors have applied to other callings, but no doors have opened for them to leave. For purposes only God knows, the one who governs providence has in mind for them to stay longer than they'd like. In my own restlessness I've sometimes turned not only to the Christmas shepherds for mentoring but also to the exiles in Jeremiah 29. First, I do so to remind myself that, in comparison to these ancestors of the faith, having to stay put where I am isn't the level of suffering I might sometimes and mistakenly imagine that it is. Second, it is to learn what it means to follow God in a place I desire to leave.

In Jeremiah 29, two different kinds of preachers are giving sermons to exiles. The one is Jeremiah. Jeremiah speaks from God. He tells the exiles that they will have to reimagine life where they are. They aren't going anywhere else for seventy years. This means that all but the babies born at the time will have passed away and finished their lives. The babies will have lived most of their lives by the time a chance to go back "home" arrives. This message is hard to take.

Another group of preachers is saying the opposite. "Don't put down roots!" they are saying. "God wouldn't keep you in exile like this!" "He is going to get you out of here!" "Dream, fidget, pack; this place is temporary; get ready to move!"

Which church would you prefer to attend if you were in exile? I think I'd prefer not to listen to Jeremiah, too. In fact, all of my life a verse from this passage has been quoted to cast a vision for my future and yours. "For I know the plans I have for you," says the Lord, "plans for welfare and not for evil, to give you a future and a hope" (Jer. 29:11).

What I failed to realize as I take up this wonderful promise is that almost everyone who originally heard it knew that they would never experience its fulfillment in Jerusalem, where they wanted to be. They had to grapple instead with the truth that the future and the hope for them with God would take place right where they were in exile—where they would live and die. Their great-grandchildren would experience the fullness of the future and the hope back in Jerusalem. The next generation would get to move, but not them. What does it mean for us if the future and the hope that God has for our welfare means that we will have to trust him right where we are?

They want to leave, but God will be with them in the city where they are. Each day they will look afresh to God in order to cultivate a place to live, do their work, love, marry, cultivate a family heritage, and actually seek the welfare of the city they want to leave as they cultivate a life of prayer within it (Jer. 29:5–7).

This means that God will be with them to sustain them and to teach them what it means to walk with him amid obstacles they'd rather not contend with.

- *Limits.* They will have a life in which they cannot be everywhere in general and nowhere in particular. Not only will they learn to decide what they will do, but they will have to come to terms with what they will not do.

- *Ambitions.* They will learn how to reorient their ambitions to the welfare of God's glory among their neighbors, in the ordinary of life, for the good of their place.

- *Frustrations.* They will have to bear with imperfections, annoyances, dislikes, and hardships.

- *Emotions.* They will learn that what makes us glad, sad, mad, or frightened cannot easily be solved solely by geographic movement.

- *Critical spirit.* They will be tempted to connect the dots of everything that is wrong. They will learn gratitude in this place.

- *Sufferings.* They will have to be in the same place as people who have hurt them or whom they have hurt or gossiped about. They will learn savvy and healing in this place.

- *Time and measurements of progress.* Seventy years (they will learn patience in this place).

Exulting in Monotony

But how do we return day by day to congregations and situations we feel restless to leave?

To return to this community is to hurt. How do I return to forgive or to endure narratives about me among some?

There are places that bore me here. When I see them, I feel that I already have. How do I return into boredom?

There are thoughts, emotions, and histories here. When I hear them, I'm overwhelmed. How do I return to what I cannot fix?

There is beauty here, and hope; the longing for redemption, and purpose. How do I return without overlooking these gifts because of my hurt, my boredom, and my inability?

Such questions start arguments with me. Then I look out my window into Webster Groves or Henryville or wherever we are. "The Lord is my shepherd," we can say. "My shepherd is a returning one. He returns here too. He takes me by the hand or carries me into the day, again and again and again. He returns, and we find hope in his company here. He is teaching us to "exult in monotony." Not all at once, but over time.

> Because children have abounding vitality . . . they always say, "Do it again"; and the grown-up person does it again until he is nearly dead. For grown-up people are not strong enough to exult in monotony. But perhaps God is strong enough to exult in monotony. It is possible that God says every morning, "Do it again" to the sun; and every evening, "Do it again" to the moon. It may not be automatic necessity that makes all daisies alike; it may be that God makes every daisy separately, but has never got tired of making them.[5]

I am slowly beginning to picture those Christmas shepherds as if years later they sat around the fire in the cool of a late evening—children and grandchildren staring into the crackle and flicker with drowsy eyes and ready for bed.

Glory had not delivered them from the daily grind. It had not delivered them from Herod killing every two-year-old male, or Roman occupation, or a corrupt church that would in the end yell, "Crucify!" Seeing the glory did not deliver them from this.

And yet an aged shepherd stokes the embers and says, "Did your old grandpa ever tell you about the time the angels—" Suddenly a chorus of grandchildren interrupts. Rolling their eyes, they moan, "Yes, Papa, we've heard that story before, many times!"

The old shepherd stokes the burning bark. He pauses and looks up and into their young eyes. His smile only broadens. "Let me tell you again," he'll say. And as the young ones moan, tired from this exulting in the same old thing, the aged man demonstrates his absence of fatigue. With awe and memory in his voice, and an ache in his back from the long day, he begins to retell the history. "It was an ordinary night, and we were watching our flocks," he says.

And so an exaltation amid the monotony rises. Worship, hope, and testimony refuse to quit. As he speaks, the old man is looking at the daisies again, and the same old, same old is bringing life to his routine. For a moment, I feel his joy among the sheep. His kids will grow up and wonder. Something larger than this worn tent and long days had put a fire in Gramps's heart and life into his eyes. It is almost as if he had some news, as if God were with him, here among the sheep pens on this unforgiving hillside, unknown by the world but known by God.

Coming Full Circle

A statement from old Samuel Rutherford has become a companion of mine. Confined to one place by the authorities of his day because of his faith, he wrote letters.

> The Great Master Gardener, the Father of our Lord Jesus Christ, in a wonderful providence with his own hand, planted me here, where by his grace, in this part of his vineyard, I grow; and here I will abide till the great master of the vineyard think fit to transplant me.[6]

I spoke about such things to Mamaw before she died. We sat in old chairs, in Henryville.

"For a long time I've been trying to get away from here," I said. "Now it seems I'm sad for the distance and the absence."

"Well," she said, looking through the walls like they were windows, "sounds like you've come full circle."

That is what roots require of a person who is nowhere in particular. He must first come full circle and there find the grace to say "Do it again" to the mundane beauties around him. We must learn to tell old stories in familiar places among a people we grow thoroughly to know. We must believe that this is enough to give life meaning. How can we learn how to do this returning work except through him who knew the names of trees? He who called you to where you are declares that you needn't repent of being in one place at one time. You needn't repent of doing only a long, small work in an extraordinary but unknown place. Standing long in one place for a while allows the roots to deepen. It allows pastors to become pastors. Slowly the shade grows and a life gives. It is Jesus *of Nazareth* who walks with you.

6

Fix It All

I have seen a man on the bank of the river buried up to his knees in mud and some men came to give him a hand to help him out, but they pushed him further in up to his neck.

BENEDICT WARD

Pastors are returning ones.

Sometimes we return to ashes, the tearing of clothes.

Sometimes we return to growls and teeth murderous within the shadows of torches.

We clench our fists. We target our sword for the enemy's ear.

"Put down your blade," says the master surrounded by wolves.

No wonder we want to run.

Broken Porches

There she lay on the front porch, curled up in a ball, barefoot and in pajamas, leaning fetal into the aluminum screen door. Her crying mom kept the door shut, having been urged by her husband to keep Lori out. Exasperated, the dad was trying force to fix the situation with "tough love." As for me, two other elders and I had been walking the streets of the neighborhood searching for Lori.

"She had run away again" is all we knew. Our search ended on the front porch. There Lori lay, locked out in her tears, and there we stood in ours.

Somehow I had not imagined that ministry in Jesus's name would mean that my life would be lived among such porches. I'm not sure why. A shepherd carries out his work among the weak, the sick, the injured, the straying, and the lost (Ezek. 34:4–5). A shepherd, in contrast to a hired hand, learns to do life among wolves, because this is what sheep do. He cares for them in these dangers (John 10:12–13). In his book *Strong at the Broken Places*, Richard Cohen puts it plainly: "We the injured are everywhere."[1]

I also had no idea that shepherds can try to avoid days of injury in order to promote their own safety and advancement. If a shepherd's aversion to broken things, his impatience with this kind of intrusion into his day, gets challenged, he can become forceful and harsh even with his flock (Ezek. 34:4).

But I now understand the injury and the attempt to control it, even if by harsh means. There on porches of everywhere injury, we can feel out of control and are sorely tempted to strive for something like omnipotence—the possession of unlimited and immediate power. "When [Eve] saw that the tree was good . . . , she took of its fruit" (Gen. 3:6).

So on broken porches there is little wonder that the Serpent's pledge would glitter and shine into preference. "You will be like God," the Serpent promised (Gen. 3:5). "You will not surely die," the Serpent hissed (v. 4). As a pastor, I want this kind of promise on the porch, and if I'm not careful, I will take of its cursed fruit. I can be god on the porch for them. I can fix them. "All is not this bad," I can tell them. "You will surely not die," I will say. "I will make this go away for you." Anything I can grab and eat or say or quote will do, anything to make me feel like I'm doing something constructive amid my helplessness. I scratch and claw to be omnipotent on the porch. I try to use strategies other than the gospel to fix all the broken things. All of us do.

Multiplying Words

Amid the injury we sometimes keep saying, "You're not supposed to do that." When preaching about David's sin, for example, my tendency was to say, "See what he did? Now don't you do that." But the problem was, of course, that David did sin already and so had many of those listening to me at the moment. So then what? Likewise, when in personal pastoral care, what can you say there on the porch as you stand with your Bible? We can say, "Don't be here!" "You shouldn't do this!" all we'd like. The problem is that everyone already is and already has. Now what? Is there any gospel hope?

Impatient for an answer and a remedy, we begin to multiply words. Consequently, someone like Job not only has to endure all that ails him; he must also deal with the flurry of texts, e-mails, letters, and phone calls of those trying to fix him in God's name.

Proverbs reminds us to look out our windows and to listen to what the real world can sound like (Prov. 7:6–23). The sights and sounds can be tragic, such as in a living room of a ministry coordinator and her husband. It is not a porch, but the damage remains.

"I'm not a Christian anymore!" he yells to her.

"You don't have to follow Jesus for us to remain married and find a good life," she responds. "I'm yours; I'm committed to you. We can get counseling. We can ask for help," she assures him.

"I'm not going to counseling together, and I'm not going to ask for help, especially from God," he declares. "I'm tired of the hypocrisy of churches. I hate this life," he retorts.

"I'll resign tomorrow," she pleads. "I don't have to be in ministry. Where do you want to go? We can go anywhere and start over," she begs. "I love you," she says.

"But I don't love you, and I never have," he retorts. "I don't want to be with you. I never have."

She is silent. Her words begin to falter. Maybe as you listen in, your words begin to fail you too.

"For me this marriage ended ten years ago," he reveals.

"You don't mean that," she mutters. "I can't believe that is true," she mumbles. You notice that she almost says the next words to herself rather than to him. "What about our kids, our memories, our life together over these years?"

"I need some air," he says and gets up from the couch. "I'm done with this."

At that moment, when her words fail, you watch her do something she has never done in fifteen years of marriage.

What does a baseball pitcher do when the other team hits his best pitch? Where does the "little engine that could" turn when she faces a mountain larger than all the others and too steep to overcome? What happens when the little engine can't? Having no answer, seeing him walk away, wordless to stop him, she stands up, grabs him, and tries physically to block his way. He moves one way, and so does she. Words dissolve into the force of will.

"I'm not letting you go!" she shouts.

"Let me through!" he yells and begins to push.

Conscience calls to her. She lets him through but then gives in to multiplying words again. She follows him in a chase down the hall, through the living room to the front door.

"Leave me alone!" he yells and then slams the door behind him.

"I'm not leaving you!" she bellows through the door.

"That's just it!" he shouts as he walks to the car. "I'm leaving you!"

Throwing Bible Words About

In the days that follow, you watch as friends, family members, and church folks multiply words. "You've let your looks go. You just need to get pretty and he will notice you more," another says to her.

Now the Bible words get multiplied. "He just needs to know what the Bible says and do it," one minister says to her. We can be tempted to hurl verses at other people almost as an incantation. We sometimes act as though there is power in speaking the words themselves, like a wizard reciting her spells. Get the words spoken correctly and the spell works. Misspeak the syllables and the spell won't work.

But the presence of things we cannot control or immediately fix reminds us that though the Bible is God's revelation, it in itself is not his magic remedy. It lights our path by his Spirit, but it cannot always shield us from what he shows us there. Only the Christ that the Bible verses reveal can do this.

Mark this down, won't you? One of the first signs that we are approaching the borders of attempting omnipotence is this: we believe that another is choosing a course of action because he or she simply isn't clear on what is right. Therefore, we believe that if we just work hard enough to explain what is right, then he or she will obviously and immediately do the right thing. No one was more plain, true, reasonable, and clear than Jesus, and they crucified him. Clarity matters a great deal. But clarity can't always solve or fix the broken things.

Imagine what the porch that morning would have become if we had believed that the best hope for that girl, her mom, and her dad amid the ruins was our formula of words, our multiplied pontifications choking out the space, the ache, and the silence? Job's friends got it right when they sat silent with him in the ashes. The damage began when they spoke. Jesus will sit in the ashes on the broken porches of our lives and teach us how to trust him more than our multiplied words.

Raising Our Voices and Pointing Our Fingers

As words fail to solve the problem, those involved start to get louder and target character. Job was not above needing correction and growth. But the character attacks made by Job's friends were misguided and cruel.

Fix-it-alls begin to think something like this: *This situation or person couldn't possibly be what it appears to be. We have quoted the Bible and made our arguments. Things should be fixed by now.*

There must be some hidden mischief here. We need to speak some more, but this time, louder and more accusatory. When this happens, we become like one who talks louder to a blind person or raises his voice at a foreigner who speaks a different language.

So now imagine again the situation of the director of ministry. Perhaps some men and women become red-faced finger pointers and call her a hypocrite. They maneuver to find some hidden debauchery in her life, tidbits and morsels for conversations and prayers.

She warrants blame. She needs more growth and change than she knows. But her sins in this case, you see, are not of the talk-show variety. She has no gossip-magazine scandal hidden in her closets. Her sins and limits do not justify her husband's leaving. Yet a community of Jesus, behind closed doors, is tempted to whisper dark speculations in meetings opened with prayer. So sometimes the porch isn't enough. There must be dirt beneath it. Impatient with unfixed things, we fill the space with speed of thought and speculation. We create foul scenarios and speak them.

"Did you have an affair?" someone asks her. "Are you a nag? Are you misusing the kids? What did you do to cause him to leave and to wreck your ministry?"

It is easier for us to handle an illness when it has a clear name and a precise cause. Sitting in the doctor's office amid undiagnosed days of "I don't know" is much more difficult. We hate the feelings that come with unfixable and uncontrollable moments. We do not know how to do a day with unfixed feelings, so we flail about and knock the dishes off the counters instead. At least we are exerting our power, we justify. We feel like we are doing something.

Writing a long, prosaic treatise e-mail punctuated by words placed in ALL CAPS might feel empowering too. But in the end this has as little power as reasoned words to fix what ails us. Imagine how we would have handled the porch that morning if we had believed that ALL CAPS treatises would untrouble and control it? Imagine if we had projected onto the girl, the mom, and the dad worse things than were actually there and therefore filled that already wrecked porch with the addition of our pointing fingers?

Fear and Intimidation

We can then begin to practice fear and intimidation as a leadership or pastoral care strategy. We can begin to yell, threaten, verbally or physically cajole, or even silent-treatment those on the porch.

The problem is that fear and intimidation work as long as gospel healing isn't our goal. I remember a ministry leader who was struggling with a personal crisis. An elder was charged with this ministry leader's care and formed an official delegation to meet with the ministry leader "to learn how they could pastorally care for him." Even though pastoral care formed the stated goal, the meeting collapsed into an interrogation, which ended with accusations and harsh words on everyone's part. The elder shared with me that he felt so sorry about that situation as he looked back on it. He said he had given in to the pressure of knowing that others involved were going to ask him very tough questions. So he had to make sure that nothing was left unturned in order to appease them. With their examination of him in his mind, he actually pointed at the man needing care and, with red-faced intensity, called him a hypocrite. I know this temptation well. Most of us in ministry do. Seeking someone's approval in our imagination or in reality, rather than Jesus's gospel, we get tripped up.

The point, of course, is that fear, intimidation, and threat will not fix a girl with anorexia in a fetal position on the porch while her mother and father avalanche with anxiety.

Pause here, won't you? Reread that last sentence.

Defensiveness

Defensiveness doesn't help us either. My defensiveness has come mostly in the form of emotional blasts—with tears, pleadings, and strong statements. Others defend by calm record keeping. Record keepers defend themselves in the way that I imagine the clergy in the good Samaritan story might have. Theirs was not a sin of commission—something they did. Theirs was the sin of omission—something they did not do. Leaving the broken man beaten by the side of the road, they could have easily defended themselves. They could have readily shown that they had done all their duty that day and never drawn attention to the beaten man. After all, his presence did not fall into their normal responsibilities. If someone did discover the broken man, the record keeper could have shown that they did nothing wrong to the man and justified why they respectively handled him the way they did.

The first kind of defensiveness, emotional blasting, is easy to see and makes others squirm to retake control. The second kind, record keeping, functions to keep everyone more comfortable, more apparently in control with detailed defense, so our ability to recognize this gospel substitute takes much longer.

Either way, defensiveness only proves the point of our brokenness and exaggerates our faults in the eyes of others, particularly if those others already see what they want to be true about us rather than what actually is true about us. Defensiveness has no power to heal.

I sit for a while with a friend. "Anger does not bring about the kingdom of God," he gently says to me. We sit in the silence sipping tea. We sit in the ashes and wait together. We wait for Jesus. Gradually, he gives the stamina to be quiet when slandered, silent when gossiped about, entrusting our reputations more and more to him and less and less to our words, emotions, or record keeping.

You were never meant to repent because you can't fix everything. You are meant to repent because you've tried. Even if we could be god for people and fix it all, the fact remains that Jesus often does not have the kind of fixing in mind that you and I want.

The Inconsolable Things

You cannot fix "the inconsolable things." The inconsolable things are identified first by the "cannots" of Jesus's teaching. For example, no matter who we are, "no one can serve two masters," no one (Matt. 6:24). Even if we are wise and knowledgeable by his grace, there are still things and seasons in our lives that we "cannot bear . . . now" (John 16:12). No matter how strong of a will a person has, "the branch cannot bear fruit by itself" (John 15:4). No matter how many oaths we take or how much we spin words into boast, we "cannot make one hair white or black," Jesus says (Matt. 5:36).

These cannots from Jesus teach us that sickness, death, poverty, and the sin that bores into and infests the human being will not be removed on the basis of any human effort, no matter how strong, godly, or wise that effort is. This is why Jesus teaches us that the faith of a mustard seed can move a mountain and "nothing will be impossible for you" (Matt. 17:20). So we bring faith to what troubles us. And according to Jesus it would seem that there is nothing in the world we can't fix if we just have the smallest seed of faith. But this is not the conclusion Jesus draws for us. Though nothing will be impossible for us with faith, "you always have the poor with you," Jesus says (Matt. 26:11). The paradox emerges. When it comes to poverty, there is no knockout punch or decision in your favor. You must step into the ring with faith, knowing that you will not win in the way you want to.

We also have no power to produce the increasing things. By "increasing things," I mean the fruit that we by our ministries hope to produce. Don't get me wrong. We can do meaningful pastoral work among the mattering things, but only God can give the increase (1 Cor. 3:6–7). Jesus teaches us that the power to give salvation is inconsolable as it relates to us. We cannot give people the new birth with God (John 3:3–5). We cannot justify someone, make her righteous, sanctify her, give her adoption, convict her of sin, or change her heart (Luke 19:27; 1 Cor. 12:3). There is nothing we can do in ministry that does not require God to act, if true fruit is to be produced (John 15:5). Everything pastors hope will take place in a person's life with God remains outside the pastor's own power.

We also cannot fix the absence of peace the way people often want us to. Why? Because Jesus gives peace but not the way the world does (John 14:27).

I met Steve years earlier at my first Bible study at Grand Village Retirement Home. He was the only one who attended my first day. I was nervous and pushed to say a prayer to end the meeting quickly. But this Purple Heart recipient had other ideas on his mind. "Father, I've not been to church in over fifty years," he said to me. I was not Catholic, but I was a "Father" to this ninety-year-old. "God could never forgive me for all the things I've done," he said, as he stared past me into a world that pained him. That day, grace gave me words to speak of Jesus and his forgiveness. Jesus drew Steve to himself.

Now, here Steve was in the hospital. His hands were tied down because he kept tearing the tubes out of his arms. He was caught in a hallucinatory world. He told me to watch out for the postman standing at the edge of his bed waiting to do me harm. I assured Steve that I was okay. I told Steve that I loved him. He gave no indication that he heard me. He was fidgety and groaning in the world he was imagining. I sat for a long while. I sang. I prayed. All the while Steve didn't recognize me. Then, as I was leaving, I leaned over and said, "I love you, Steve."

Steve shot me a look. The fidget, the moans, and the illusions collapsed from his eyes. For a moment he saw me clearly. "I heard ya the first time!" he declared. Then for an instant more, we looked at each other and saw each other. Then the moment left, and his turmoil returned. Yet love asserted itself there amid the hallucinations, the tied hands, and the fading mind. There is a kind of peace that Jesus gives. It goes where other kinds of power will not. It does what other kinds of power cannot.

His power is found when singing "Amazing Grace" to a woman in hospice, wheezing in the dark for breath. Singing of his grace makes the lungs relax, and the breathing eases. Death will not stop. Inconsolable things will not quit, not yet, not for a while longer. But grace has come. Something more powerful than death hums softly alongside her and holds her hands.

We cannot do everything that needs to be done, which means that Jesus will teach us to live with the things we can neither control nor fix. We will want to resist Jesus and act as if we are omnipotent, but we will harm others and ourselves when we try. Others will also resist Jesus. Using his name, they will praise or critique us, promote or overlook us, according to their desire that we fix everything for them and that we do it immediately. But they will have to learn too that only Jesus can fix everything and that there are some things Jesus leaves unfixed for his glory.

This feels excruciating at times. We enter situations every day knowing that we have no control and that our only true hope in which we place our confident faith is that God will do in this awkward silence what he alone can do according to his ability and love. No wonder we hurry about trying to fix it all. It is so much less humiliating to move about, speak words, make plans, and hurry into action than to wait for a while longer and see; or to fall to the floor, tear our clothes, and enter the weeping with people. But to enter the weeping with people is what Jesus leads us to. Waiting and seeing what God will do is no waste of time.

Our Winsome Harming

King Herod would not agree with this kind of power. His strategies for solving problems made problems go away but healed nothing (Matt. 2:18). King Herod was no "wounded healer."[2]

Perhaps we are nicer than King Herod. The fact is, when we strive to fix it all apart from Jesus, even nice ministry leaders can become winsome harmers. We join a long line.

- Job's friends, lacking sincere empathy, thought they knew more than they did. In their hands, doctrine excused ignorance. Correctness justified a cruel word. Truth, we learn from them, can be used unfeelingly and foolishly. Truth can be used to hurt people. The mandate to speak truth with love mutated into "I'll tell it like it is."

- The shepherds of Ezekiel 33 used ministry to manipulate people in order to gain status, comfort, and reputation. They left the broken, the lost, and the harassed to the wolves.

- The elder brother of the prodigal son represented the Pharisees (Luke 15:11–32). These Bible teachers justified ingratitude and bitterness in the name of standing for righteousness. They gracelessly pounded people with religious virtues.

- The religious leaders in the good Samaritan story (Luke 10:25–37) had no concept of love for neighbor when they were "off duty."

- In fact, for any of us in the vocation of ministry, it is sobering to realize that the harshest things Jesus ever said (like the prophets who foreshadowed Jesus) were for the ministry leaders of his day (Matt. 23:1–36).

Peruse the heroes of our faith, and the temptation for genuine leaders to winsomely harm others and offend God is no less prominent.

- We know about Noah's drunken debacle as well as his courage and faith.

- We rightly honor Abraham's faith, while rightly remembering the fact that selfish fear could get the best of him.

- Moses murdered. He shrank back. His temper squandered his opportunity to physically step into the Promised Land. Yet he also believed and courageously led.

- We sing the psalms of a man after God's own heart. But this man also did terrible deeds and at times made tragic choices far beneath his calling and the grace given him.

- Jonah raised his fists at grace.

- James and John wanted to call down fire and consume those who disregarded Jesus.

- Paul teaches us. But God made sure that we receive Paul's teaching and integrity while knowing Saul of Tarsus's bitter story.

- Peter exalts Christ for us. But we are not gullible regarding the kind of cowardly sin that Peter exemplified when Jesus was arrested.

Somehow I thought the contours of my life and ministry would look distant from these biblical leaders and heroes. I thought that I would not make their mistakes or share their vulnerabilities. But standing on that porch, I am a broken pot and without any superhero cape. We're all broken, earthen vessels on that porch—the mom behind the door, the dad on the phone, the two elders with me, and the girl piled in the ruins.

We would get Lori up off that porch that day, go on into our normal routines of chores, food, prayer, Bible reading, music lessons for our kids, and sleeping. But the thing that brought Lori to the porch in the first place would remain unrepaired that night and for many, many nights to come. Each of us, therefore, would have to learn how to live each day with each other and none of it or us fixed.

Mounting an Offense

In her remarkable memoir regarding her ongoing battle with chronic rheumatoid arthritis, Mary Felstiner asks: "How can a soul rise to the occasion of illness?"[3] By "illness," Mary meant the diseased wrecking of one's body into disrepair. By inquiring how a soul rises to this occasion, she meant choosing and learning to live stubbornly, vibrantly, and lovingly onward within the carnage that once was her fingers or legs.

Her disease is a sadist to joints and bones. It pulverizes them with a grin. It wrenches them out and yanks at them. It twists them into a mangle while chuckling. So when I hear her call us to "rise

101

to the occasion," I recognize that she intends to fight. But her way of fighting startles me. "At least now I know what the job is," she says. "Mount an offense when no match is mine to win."[4]

This past year I received a letter from one of the elders who had stood with me on that porch that morning those years ago. I learned from the letter that Lori's life, all these years later, had healing in it. What he described regarding the grace that found her and holds her still, amazed me into tears.

How did Jesus's peace calm her life? To be honest, I'm not fully sure. No large, notable, efficient, and speedy answer is available. The only things that we could muster were small, overlooked things over a long period of time. One of the elders wrote an e-mail once a week to Lori throughout her trauma. Every Monday it simply began, "Good morning." In it he spoke of the beauty he saw in her and the grace of Jesus that he prayed for her.

Another elder allowed Lori to live with his family for a while as her family sought grace to make it through. There was some counseling. There were lots of tears and setbacks. Psalms were cried and poured out.

A lot of time went by, years of unfixed days with no seeming answers or remedies. So how did the healing come amid such inconsolable things? How will Jesus continue on with her amid the inconsolable things that are still hers to navigate?

I can't really say. In fact, as I think back to that porch all I know for sure is this: the match wasn't ours to win. It was his. And he did.

7

Know It All

Anyone who thinks that he has understood the divine scriptures or any part of them, but cannot by his understanding build up this love of God and neighbor, has not yet succeeded in understanding them.

AUGUSTINE

I had just given Eric his first Bible. He had only prayed in Jesus four or five times during his life (and this in the last two days!).

An elder had stopped by to pick up something for Sunday school class. "Hey, Jason!" I said to the elder.[1] "I'd like you to meet Eric, a new Christian. We are meeting for the first time today. I just gave Eric his first Bible."

The elder shook the new convert's hand and said hello. What he said next stunned me. "So, Eric," he said. "What is your opinion of Westminster Larger Catechism Question 109?"

Eric smiled blankly and looked at me.

I remember that long-ago moment. I look at it like a mirror that warns me and raises a question. How do we get to the place where we forget that there was a time that we too didn't know what the Gospel of John was, much less how to find it in the Bible or how to read it when we did? What is it about how we Christians sometimes view growth in knowledge that enables us to belittle or demean or judge or confound or overwhelm a person who is opening his first Bible for the first time? The haunting answer is that the Serpent's temptation still whispers to us: "You will be like God, *knowing . . .*" (Gen. 3:5).

We are tempted to something like omniscience—the ability to know everything. But you were never meant to repent because you don't know it all. You are meant to repent because you've tried.

Apprentices

In his *The Sorcerer's Apprentice*, Goethe writes about a master who leaves his young student in charge. Ambitious, the young apprentice surmises that he is ready to fill his master's shoes because he has "memorized what to say and do."[2] Those familiar with the famed Disney version of this poem will likely remember the frenzy and damage that results. Though he tried to imitate the tasks of his master, he neither embodied the ways of his master nor understood the depth of the powers that confronted him. Therefore, all his efforts only worsened his plight until finally he humbled himself, begged the master's return, and received in surrender the master's gracious and powerful rescue.

The poet's point is obvious. Trying to access the power of a vocation by mere memory and incantation will shortly make a mess of things.

The Bible agrees. Several itinerant preachers had watched the apostle Paul cast out demons and perform miracles in Jesus. They took stock of themselves and surmised that they could likewise do what Paul had done. So when they happened upon such evil spirits, these preachers mimicked what they had observed in Paul.

"I adjure you by the Jesus whom Paul proclaims," one of them cried out. To which the demon retorted, "Jesus I know, and Paul I recognize, but who are you?" Immediately, the preachers who tried to practice what they had memorized but not embodied were overpowered and fled the scene naked and wounded (Acts 19:11–16).

The demon was astute. It recognized that no matter how much

the preachers' words and actions resembled those of Jesus, the quality of Jesus's authority, life, and teaching was absent.

We too can misuse knowledge in this way. In my first days of seminary we students of an intensive Greek class gathered for a break each day to pray for one another. Not many days into this daily routine of gathering for prayer beneath the shade of a summer tree, an upperclassman walked boldly toward us and rebuked us:

> Brothers, I warn you! You are obviously proud and stubborn. It is obvious you want the rest of us to see how spiritual and holy you are. I know. I too was once a new student like yourselves. I too wanted to show off to everyone like you do now. But I was wrong and so are you! Jesus calls us to "go to our closets" to pray. You call yourselves future pastors? You need to repent!

If there was light for our path from the goodness of the Scripture our brother quoted, we had a hard time seeing it. His use of "light" made us squint our eyes. If there was something beautiful and redemptive about who he had been when he first started seminary, we couldn't see by the light he was trying to offer us.

We objected, "Are we justified in passionately rebuking people without discerning whether they know any better or as if they have nothing to learn to help them grow? Is Jesus against anyone ever praying in front of someone else? Didn't Jesus pray in front of his disciples and in the presence of others?"

For all of our mutual knowledge of the Bible, I don't think we apprentices helped each other to see very much at all that day. A flashlight shone directly into someone's eyes makes seeing harder, not easier. A flashlight misused can actually rob us of the light it is meant to provide.

Puffing Up

Knowledge meant to help us often only puffs us up (1 Cor. 8:1–2), and misuse of zeal is no different. In America, potato-chip bags are puffed up. But when the bag is opened, it deflates. What looked like a full bag of chips was actually a bag filled mostly with air. As genuine believers in Jesus we are susceptible to becoming puffed up and full of hot air in these ways (among others), especially pastors.

Our zeal with our newness to the faith can exaggerate our knowledge and puff us up (1 Tim. 3:6).

Our zeal for theological controversy, debate, and discussion to demonstrate our superior intellect or persuasive ability over others puffs us up too (1 Tim. 6:4).

Dr. Well-Known Preacher was a helpful pastor who sometimes passionately preached with a prophetic edge about suffering for the gospel. There was for a few years a contingency of students who fashioned themselves as his disciples. They listened to his sermons, read his books, and attended his conferences (though to my knowledge none of them knew Dr. Well-Known Preacher personally except for a handshake at a conference). With red-faced passion, they preached in Bible class about suffering. They sought to lead more ascetic lives on their seminary campus. But by adopting just one aspect of their celebrity mentor's message without the context and personal experience of his years of pastoral travail for people, they actually hurt fellow students, misjudged professors, and strongly criticized both, and this in the name of God.

They seemed blind to the fact that for all their zeal, they had actually only preached four sermons in their lives. They glossed over the fact that they had never served a day as a pastor in a church. They dismissed the truth that what they had learned only yesterday in class, the professor teaching them had been seeking to live out in life and ministry before they were even born.

Jonathan Edwards noted, "There is nothing that belongs to Christian experience that is more liable to a corrupt mixture than zeal."[3] It is not that we desire less zeal. On the contrary, a life and ministry devoid of earnestness is like a heater that sits in a damp room on a cold day but does not work. We plug it in, all goose bump and tremble, frigid toes needing to be warmed, but no help comes. Thank the Lord for zealous young men and women!

But a fire can't safely warm us unless it is the proper distance from us. Get too close in the name of warmth, and we get burned. Our zeal is meant to be derived "according to knowledge" (Rom. 10:2).

When Jesus gives his "Woe!" to those who misuse the key of knowledge, Jesus highlights the signs we exhibit when knowledge has gone wrong.

Our Bible knowledge leaves us illiterate in terms of the interior workings of our souls (Luke 11:37–40).

The schooling we gain leaves us ignorant of actual love for God (Luke 11:42–44).

For all our scholarship and erudition we remain unpracticed with neighbor love, humility, wisdom, and the deeds that truly honor God (Luke 11:45–51).

We are intelligent with Bible passages but without know-how in terms of the sense or meaning of these passages as they are in Jesus. In fact, Jesus tells Bible handlers elsewhere that they know the Bible but not the one to whom the Bible points (John 5:39).

> Woe to you lawyers! For you have taken away the key of knowledge. You did not enter yourselves, and you hindered those who were entering. (Luke 11:52)

According to Jesus, when it came to describing the door of God, such Bible teachers were accredited door experts. They spent their days gathering people to look at this door, to painstakingly memorize every line, crack, corner, color, and carving. And yet, according to Jesus, these Bible teachers and their congregations possessed an expert knowledge of a door they could not open. Ironically and tragically, by their knowledge they actually made inoperable the very key that they themselves proposed to know all about. A wise old pastor was right: "It is possible for us to develop a false notion of knowledge."[4]

We may attend a local Bible study for years. We may finish a seminary degree or fulfill one year in a local-church apprentice program. But this does not mean that one is able to illumine rather than blind, to warm rather than scorch.

Knowing in Sorts

I gave up on the moon once. It was early evening. The clouds had taken the night off. Commanding center stage, the moon confidently lit up the dark hemisphere. The kids and I watched the performance through our van windows.

"What do you think, Caleb?" I asked. "What do you think of that moon?"

Caleb is my youngest. He looked intently into the sky. The moonlight reached through the window and lightly touched his left cheek. Then little Caleb surprised us all.

"Broke, Daddy," he said.

With sudden urgency, he thrust his arm and pointed with his finger out the window. "The moon broken," he clarified.

I looked again through the window up at center stage. "Oh, Caleb," I explained. "The moon isn't broken. It's a crescent moon."

Caleb did not understand the word *crescent*, but it sounded monster-like. His face fell with seriousness. With furrowed brows he pleaded with me, "Daddy, fix it!"

We all laughed out loud. "Daddy can't fix the moon, buddy," I chuckled. "It's too far away and too big." Caleb looked out the window again and then back at me.

Without hesitation Caleb looked hard at me and said, "Daddy, go there. Daddy, go there and fix moon!"

As my eyes met the expectation in his, I was confounded. I had identified the moon as "crescent" and stopped further observation. But Caleb wasn't satisfied with my explanation of *the sort* of moon it was. The luminary was shadowed, and little Caleb was trying to account for the shadow. What I called "crescent," Caleb called "broken." He wanted it to be made well again.

The way I saw the moon, named its kind, and dismissed further attention from it (in contrast to how Caleb looked beyond its sort to the moon itself) exposes another problem with knowing.

> If this man were a prophet, *he would have known who and what sort* of woman this is who is touching him, for she is a sinner. (Luke 7:39)

It is not that knowing in sorts is wrong in itself. This Pharisee correctly identified the sort this woman was according to the Bible (Prov. 7:1–21). Jesus likewise had this knowledge. He too rightly identified the woman as a sinner (Luke 7:48). As it related to the sort of woman she was, the teacher and the pupil were agreed.

But take note. Because we are right on one thing never means that we are right about everything or even about what matters most.

True repentance is happening right in front of this Pharisee, and he does not account for it (v. 48). He either does not have a category for repentance that equals his category for sin, or he does but has no experience with applying it.

For all his God-knowledge, this man's relational treatment of Jesus is profoundly impoverished (vv. 44–46). He either does not have an equally palpable category for personal hospitality, or he does but cannot or will not apply it.

This woman is seeking forgiveness right in front of him, and he cannot see it (vv. 41–43). Either he does not have a robust way of sorting out forgiveness, or he does but is blind to his inability to put it into practice.

True love for God and neighbor is happening right in front of him, and he despises it while remaining blind to his own absence from it (v. 47). Either he does not have a solid category for sorting out what true love for God and neighbor is, or he does but has little of it in his own being.

The Purpose of Knowing

And what but love in Christ forges the purpose of our knowledge anyway (Matt. 22:38–39)? The elder had knowledge of the

Westminster Larger Catechism. The upperclassman had knowledge of Jesus's words regarding prayer in secret. I had knowledge in six-week Greek class. But each of us struggled to relate soundly (i.e., with a resemblance of Jesus's love) to the people in front of us. The Scriptures in Jesus lead us toward "an epistemology of love, a way of knowing that is manifest in loving."[5]

> So, anyone who thinks that he has understood the divine scriptures or any part of them, but cannot by his understanding build up this love of God and neighbor, has not yet succeeded in understanding them.[6]

Over the years I've derived these questions for my Bible reading and preaching as a vaccine against this knowledge in sorts that puffs up and heats up but misses what Jesus intends.

- What does this passage show me about the loveliness of God? Or, put another way, what is it about God in this passage that calls for my love for him?

- What does this passage show me about people and about what love requires of me on their behalf?

- As one who has been shown mercy and love from God, what empowerment from him do I need to overcome my obstacles to love? What about the love of God in Jesus gives me hope and provision for my own lovelessness?

Then, if something that I read seems anything but lovely or loving, I write it down, step back, and keep in mind the lovely things that I have clearly seen on other Bible pages. Without letting go of these lovely things I ask about the text that seems unlovely to me. I begin a dialogue with the Father in Jesus about the loveliness he sees there, and in community conversation, I trust that he will show me in time by his Spirit what he sees.

Gracious Time and Time and More Time Again

Another help against our temptation to know in all the wrong ways is Jesus's way with Peter. When you look at Peter's life, when would you say that Peter "arrived," "got it," or "knew it all"?

He walks on water but worries about the storm and sinks. Yet Jesus does not act as if Peter has no faith. He acknowledges that Peter's faith is real, but "little." Jesus then invites Peter into a dialogue for learning. "Why did you doubt?" The tone isn't harsh. The rebuke isn't demeaning. The relationship isn't over. Falling short and trying are part of the training (Matt. 14:29–33).

Then Peter wrongly tries to stop Jesus from washing his feet (John 13:6–8), but this is no sin (John 13:6–8). Jesus tells us so. Jesus has room for Peter to encounter things he has no category for and has yet to learn. It is okay to say to Jesus, we don't understand (Matt. 15:15).

Then Peter declares, "You are the Christ, the Son of the living God" (Matt. 16:16). At that moment we think to ourselves, *Surely, Peter has now arrived!*

But immediately after this, we learn from Peter that a genuine profession of faith in Jesus does not dismiss remaining folly from our lives. "Get behind me, Satan!" are our Lord's words for Peter's boneheaded desire to keep Jesus from the cross (Matt. 16:23). Yet even these harsh words did not separate Jesus from Peter. Jesus did not cast him out or treat him as anything other than his true friend, follower, and brother.

Still, Peter's follies continue to abound. He declares that his faith is superior and his commitment strong (Matt. 26:33–35). He has no idea how terribly he has overestimated himself or how spiritually charged with satanic attack are his circumstances. If not for the intercession of Jesus, Peter along with the others would have been sifted like wheat (Luke 22:31). And yet Peter keeps falling asleep when Jesus asks him to watch and pray (Mark 14:37).

Then, Peter cuts off the ear of Malchus and receives Jesus's rebuke (John 18:10–11). Peter denies Jesus with cussing and blaspheming.

The rooster crows, and he weeps bitterly (Mark 16:66–72). And yet Jesus pursues him, loves him, and keeps him (Mark 16:7).

Peter hurts and feels stung by Jesus's words, and yet these very words are restoring him (John 21:15–19). Even after the resurrection, Peter hides in fear after seeing the empty tomb (John 20:10, 19–22) and later requires Paul's rebuke because of how fear got the best of him again (Gal. 2:11–14).

And yet for all this mistake making, folly, and sin, what Peter needed was gracious room to grow. Peter is neither Caiaphas nor Pontius Pilate, neither Herod nor the Pharisee who in his home judged both Jesus and the sinful woman. Jesus saw mistakes, errors, and sins in Peter. This did not count Peter out and did not mean that he deserved the same response from Jesus as these others warranted.

A question or two surfaces for us to mull over: How do you handle it when other people get things wrong? Does anyone you serve have room to make a mistake? What does it mean that as a pastor, you too need the time and time and time again of Jesus's grace?

Impatient Knowledge

Over the years, in the family of American evangelicalism to which I belong, it's been the rare environment of grace in which mistakes and sins are differentiated and in which the time needed to grow in relation to both is granted.

Imagine "Rev. Famous Author." For a long while, he has written of the gospel of Jesus truly and helpfully to many. But in his latest book or blog post Rev. Famous Author, while trying to account for the gospel in our culture, seems to go askew on a fundamental teaching. This is a genuine problem.

Apollos had this problem too. The gifted preacher of Jesus needed the gracious provision of Priscilla and Aquila to learn. They heard him preach. They gave thanks for it. They grew from it. But they at the same time invited him for dinner. They taught him things privately. They asked challenging questions personally (Acts 18:24–28). Apollos was given room to grow. His good teaching was not made void just because he got some things wrong.

We are often less patient. We take on late-night banter, blogging attacks, and tweeting daggers as if the culture, rather than Jesus, is our master. So Dr. Well-Known Preacher and Mr. National Blogger immediately and publicly castigate Rev. Famous Author and relationally disassociate from him.

Then Long-Established Scholar and Dr. Conference Speaker offer an all-or-nothing response that acts as if, by making one error, Rev. Famous Author is all and only error. This sounds more like how Jesus dealt with the Pharisees than how Jesus dealt with Peter or how Jesus had Apollos dealt with. At minimum, wisdom teaches us that time is needed to determine which posture of heart the erring brother is coming from.

I'm trying to say that there is something about our way of knowing that struggles to uphold two truths at the same time: (1) Rev. Famous Author is making a fundamental error by this aspect of his teaching; (2) Rev. Famous Author loves Jesus, has followed him faithfully for years, has helped the faithful, and needs our company and civil conversation in order to have a shot at growing. (Maybe by this kind of company and familial dialogue we might learn something too?)

I've carried the subtle idea around with me that growing in knowledge will mean that I get to depend less and control more. But Jesus indicates the opposite. The humble knows the most and knows it not.

The Know-It-All Pastor at Home

Imagine what it is like to live with your pastor if he is a know-it-all. His use of God knowledge puffs him up, and he eye-blinds you with sorting and face-scorches you with zeal. For all his Bible zeal you can't remember the last time you knew what it felt like to be understood, cherished, known, or deeply loved.

Often you've been corrected, even gently and reasonably told why you and not he got it wrong again. You can't remember the last time he kissed you with the humble dignity of saying to you: "I'm sorry. I was wrong; you were right."

We fear humble desires.

We resist being creaturely and human.

We forget who we once were and how it was that Jesus loved us and walked with us before we knew so much, even back then, when so much of what we knew was off.

Gradually a young seminary student suspects his wife's immaturity because she does not know or act in a certain theological way, even though he himself had never heard of this way until that afternoon in a class.

A pastor impatiently demands his children to know, believe, and do what it took him twenty-five or forty-five years with Jesus to know, believe, and do. How is it that his own life of mistake making has hardened rather than softened his compassion, when he himself has needed so much grace?

Conclusion

Someone will hear me saying, "Right! We don't need Bible knowledge; we just need Jesus!"

But I'm not saying this. Such a sentiment is itself a way of knowing. It is rarely wise to suggest that we can know Jesus without at least some scraps of what his words reveal to us about him.

Instead, I am trying to talk about knowing according to what Jesus says that knowing is. Our pastoral work needs this mentoring. He is the returning one, the Good Shepherd. He knows his sheep—including that woman sorted out by the Bible teacher. But in what way does he know her? He knows her by name. He calls to her, goes before her, leads her out. He is her doorway to green pastures and rest. He is with her in the midst of her troubles, needs, vulnerabilities, and dignities. He lays down his life for her (John 10:2–4). She is known in such a way that she has learned to know something too—his voice, his ways, to follow. Our hope is not that we know everything but that our Shepherd does.

"Partial Knowledge" is the name of the street on which each of us must have an address and build our lives (1 Cor. 13:12). Therefore, start each day with this admission: regarding every person, bit of creation, and circumstance that I encounter today, I must say to God, "I am in the dark," and, "I've been mentored to distort what sits before my eyes." I must remember that when I enter the pulpit, stand by a hospital bed, take a walk, or sit in my chair to counsel another, I physically see people and things always as one at dusk.

Jehoshaphat's prayer becomes ours. "We do not know what to do [Lord], but our eyes are on you" (2 Chron. 20:12).

We receive Paul's prayer and ask it afresh:

That you, being rooted and grounded in love, may have strength to comprehend with all the saints what is the breadth and length and height and depth, and to know the love of Christ that surpasses knowledge, that you may be filled with all the fullness of God. Now to him who is able to do far more abundantly than all that we ask or think. (Eph. 3:17–20)

8

Immediacy

I think the besetting sin of pastors, maybe especially
evangelical pastors, is impatience.

EUGENE PETERSON

I recently attended a regional meeting of pastors in which they
learned that 80 percent of the churches they had started over the
previous ten years had not lasted. Eight out of ten pastors spoke
once of dreams, God's work, and difference-making in our generation. They prayed and hoped and spent. Everyone cheered, planned,
and prayed. But soon after, many returned home bandaged among
the wounded.

Conversely, a few churches not only start well but they grow
numerically and fast. These few churches catch on so quickly that
their crowds create a buzz in the community. Pastors have to hire
more help and immediately. Folks have to develop more programs
and speedily. They have to scramble and race about just to keep
up with the rush of people hurrying into "the new place to be in
town." After a little while the leadership is exhausted, and the
structures that haste required aren't suitable for caring for people
over the long haul. No roots exist. The tree is top-heavy. Restruc-
turing and repositioning have to take place or else the burned-out

leaders and volunteers of the church will collapse. They have to slow down in order to keep going, but they don't know how; they never learned.

Similarly, my friend on the phone was in his third year. He was exhausted, showing signs of wear.

"I can slow down later," he said. "If I slow down now, what will happen to the ministry?"

"But if you *don't* slow down now, what will happen to the ministry?" I asked. "If you stay at your current pace, what you fear could likely happen anyway."

• • •

I share these three stories as one who remembers the dizzy spells that signified my own imminent fall. They knocked my head and spun my vision at the oddest moments. I was a lead pastor with a young family and a growing church and pursuing a PhD all at the same time. Doctors ran tests in order to detect inner ear or brain malfunctions. After months, nothing surfaced. A doctor finally asked me the question. "Is there any stress in your life?"

I think back about that now and laugh. I shake my head. Any stress? If my body was a tree, my roots were struggling to hold their ground. I was beginning to sway even on days of sky blue with no wind. Sometimes circumstances will force us to reckon with the necessity of patience for our pastoral work. We will have to surrender to the mentoring of the Spirit in his kind of fruit, or we will crash instead headlong onto the ground, dead roots exposed to the world.

What makes slowing down so difficult? It is our cravings for something other than fame-shy work, our everywhere for all, know-it-all, fix-it-all attempts to replace God, and our prayerlessness, which leaves us burdened with a load only God is meant to carry. Yes, but circumstances don't often help us much either.

Why People Leave

People ordinarily leave a church with a new pastor for one of two reasons (and often within the first two to three years of the new pastor's arrival): (1) the new pastor is not enough like the previous pastor and things are changing too much; or (2) the new pastor is too much like the previous pastor and things are not changing enough. Groups gather and talk to one another about which side they take. They reinforce their displeasure.

But other negative factors can also collide and conspire to increase these pressures.

For us, it was an economic recession that sandstormed the country. Many not-for-profits and churches were suffering. We were no exception. The elders and I were initiating conversations with pastoral staff about the possible implications for all of our jobs. Late-night meetings were becoming the norm for our leadership. We had looked at printed pages with numbered facts. We had examined taut budgets that would budge no further. We had prayed for leaving people whom we loved and prayed for staying people who were worn out. In time, we might have to make harder decisions that would impact others on our team, and we were staring wordlessly at each other.

It didn't help that I had started part-time. Our plan was that I would ease in as full-time pastor gradually over two years. This idea was noble, but it didn't work. When someone called me on Wednesday at 3:00 p.m. asking immediately to see me, I'd say, "I can call you tonight on the phone or tomorrow afternoon. If those times don't work, I can see you on Friday." The person felt offended. It was strange for them and for me, I guess, this strangeness of having to wait. They felt uncared for. I felt guilty. When immediacy is our norm, sometimes having to wait for a phone call three hours from now makes us feel overlooked. We complain.

I was preaching out of pain too, pain from many things. Years later, we've belly laughed with tears about my dirge of an Easter sermon early on. I had explored death, darkness, and pain so

119

thoroughly and miserably for twenty minutes that by the time I tried to point us to the resurrection, no one could see it. We laugh now in the grace of memory—the humbling patience of friends who stuck it out together. But it required a lot of people who had little patience for it.

Besides all this we had ironically offered a vision of patience too quickly. Going the long haul together in community felt foreign, not to mention boring. Seeing a congregation as a people with whom to do life rather than a product to mobilize, or seeing a pastor as someone to love rather than to consume for an experience, was new to most of us.

When all was said and done, 150 people left our church in three years. One hundred-fifty thousand dollars of our budget went with them. We had to let three full-time staff go. We gave several months of lead time and severance. But we all hurt. We questioned ourselves. We became the talked-about church in the community. But the talk wasn't hopeful and was often unkind. This isn't easy to overcome—not by sprinting. On the contrary, the impatient mindset of trying to do large things famously and immediately partially torpedoed us. We almost sank. Almost.

We were asking with earnest tears and humiliated hearts an important question among the mattering things: "Lord, please teach us to follow you into what it looks like to recover this sinking ship."

The Attraction of Haste

To begin, we had to become teachable to what pastoral work actually requires. Eugene Peterson finishes the quote that I noted above in this way:

> I think the besetting sin of pastors, maybe especially evangelical pastors, is impatience. We have a goal. We have a mission. We're going to save the world. We're going to evangelize everybody, and we're going to do all this good stuff and fill our churches. This is wonderful. All the goals are right. But this is

slow, slow work, this soul work, . . . and we get impatient and start taking shortcuts.[1]

"Walk," we say to my toddler son, who wants to run with his buddies beside the public pool. I tell him to slow down not because I want him to miss his mark but exactly because slowness is his best shot of actually hitting it.

So maybe we can describe *haste* as "feeling late" or "thinking we have to run." Wherever we are, it is like we are itching to leave. We have somewhere we are supposed to be, but where we are is never that place. So we constantly feel we are missing out, losing our chance, or forfeiting what we could have had if we could just get there before the hourglass sand empties out. In our case, we first had to assess why we thought we were missing out.

1) To begin with, *haste is part of the air we breathe*. Even though the word *slow* in the Bible is most often used to describe the good character of God, *slow* to most of us equals waste or disrespect.

2) *Our particular church's past*. Our church had been popular once, that is, prior to our split. We were up-and-coming in the community, and the talk was on the rise about what God was doing among us. The prayers of the people who left the comfort of a home church to start this new gospel work were being answered. But then a devastating fracture between good people ransacked much of that. So when I came, there was a palpable longing to gain back what had been lost. But by then, I was the fourth lead in six years. In my first months, five marriages broke, two groups of folks slandered and ruined relationships, and a house group imploded in a thoroughly damaging way. We were now asking ourselves hard questions and making confessions. If our popularity was truly synonymous with health, how is it that our internal relationships careened so readily into division and fracture? A longing for immediate revival and return can tempt us to say no to patience and yes to shortcuts.

3) *We were not far from the "successful" church in town*. Down the road from us is a church that grew fast and large. Its resources

are spread now throughout the city. Some thought we were on our way to being like this church. Others were saddened by how many of our folks had left to go there. Others were miffed or made insecure by how it feels to be like a small, locally owned store in the presence of a giant chain store and trying to compete as the chain store builds more and more stores around ours. Though most churches in America are not this size nor grow this fast, the rest of us are tempted to believe that their story, and not ours, is the gospel norm in the world. Measuring ourselves by the church down the road can tempt us to believe that we have fallen behind and are passed over. We start to speed up, measuring ourselves by their calling rather than ours.

4) *I was considered the real deal.* Looking back, we are humbled by the hype about me, too. The previous pastor was my friend. Our heartbeat was the same. In our community, I was a medium-sized fish in a small pond. "Dr. Eswine" had come. We all expected that great things would follow. Maybe the celebrity mind-set that infects our larger culture was tripping us up. The presence of a touted leader can tempt us to overlook what ordinary patience in pastoral work requires, no matter who we are.

5) *Our heart for the gospel exceeded our skills with the gospel.* This church is remarkable. It did what few others would. It called a single dad with care of his three children to be its pastor. Trying to back out of the search process, I had said, "I do not know how to be a single dad and a pastor at the same time." They answered, "Neither do we, but we will learn together." I will talk more about this later. But for now, it is enough to say that we were like missionaries overseas who, one year in, wonder what they were ever thinking. What the commitment actually required of all of us to love each other was more real and tangible than the grace we had dreamed of giving. Take note of this: trying to transition from a missional vision statement of neighbor love to actual neighbor love can tempt us to quit into impatience and shortcuts.

We had to find a paradigm of a different kind.

Our Marathon Need

"Let us *run with endurance*," the apostle says about "the race that is set before us" (Heb. 12:1).

A marathon is a creature that chews up those who attempt to attack it with an all-out bolt. Marathon runners also talk about "hitting the wall." Between the twentieth and twenty-third mile, legs buckle. Lungs burn. The reasons to justify quitting multiply. Cheering crowds no longer provide the inspirational fuel that they provided at earlier mile markers.

This experience does not lead marathon runners to stop running marathons or to yell with fright at anyone who says they'd like to try it, "Go away! At mile twenty-three you will want to lay down and die! Why run at all?" Instead, knowing about the wall fuels education, preparation, and training. Rather than run from it, they run toward it, having trained for what to do when it comes.

In contrast, when pastors hit walls in their first three years or at year fourteen or at year twenty, they wonder if they are called into ministry at all, as if something unique and unexpected is happening to them. When relationships, marriages, parents, new jobs, or small groups at church hit walls, their first thought is that something is wrong. They made a mistake. They need to quit.

What if, instead, we learned to name the walls ahead of time and to talk about the pace required not only to face them but to endure them, to outlast them, and to go strongly on toward the gospel finish line of our callings?

Forgetting our own marathon need, we felt the kind of stress a church planter feels in his first two years, or the stress a young pastor experiences in a rural church, or the stress a pastor with large potential and expectations senses. "I've served for two years, and we still have only twenty-five people," he says to himself. "Am I even called? Is God working at all? Should I move on to another place? Did I make a mistake in coming here?"

Our circumstances were different from that, but the underlying belief was the same. Because reality was smaller, slower, painful, imperfect, uncomfortable, and seemingly ordinary, we were asking, "Why? What happened? Are we doing something wrong?" So were those who left early.

We had actually staffed ahead of the curve. And this is where immediacy was our coach. By "the curve," we meant the numerical growth that was coming. Looking back now, we were asking ourselves, Why had we assumed the coming of a curve? Why did we feel we needed one? And why had we assumed that if it came, it would come fast?

The apostle Paul offers texts of marathon for our pastoral work. Pastors are like soldiers who endure suffering, athletes whose way of life competes according to what the rules of the race require; farmers, working hard, among the soils, weathers, and seasons. Then Paul commends us to "think over" what he says (see 2 Tim. 2:3–7). The meditating pastor must necessarily slow down too.

No wonder, as Paul sees it, we need a stamina for going long distances Christianly as we relate to friend and critic, storm and sunshine, bombast and calm. Pastors are long-distance grace runners. Congregations provide the route their marathons will take.

Patience as a Pastoral Virtue

This pastoral paradigm was bringing us face-to-face with an old joke in Christian circles. "Pray for anything except patience," the joke suggests. "You don't want to see what God will give you if you ask for that. Praying for patience is dangerous."

I've laughed and told this joke. Now I think the joke is on me. I never realized how the joke mistakenly presumes that one can follow Jesus without patience. It also assumes that God will not bother with patience in our lives unless we ask for it. I have been wrong on both counts. One assumption in the joke is true: patience is often learned within the context of trial. The trials seem like interruptions to our otherwise good lives. But more often than not, the trials become the dogs that bark at the impatience and haste that are trying to sneak into the halls of our lives. We wouldn't see the intruder lurking to harm us without such barking. And impatience does harm to us. In God's eyes, it will do more harm to us than our trials do (James 1:2–4).

We experienced relational pain amid the torrent of friends who left for different churches. We also spent hours in late-night and lunchtime discussions making decisions in our fatigue. How could we sort out the difference between friend and foe amid this swirl of complaint, pain, and freefall?

Paul apprenticed Timothy and Silvanus in this work, and we found his help.

> We urge you, brothers, admonish the idle, encourage the fainthearted, help the weak, *be patient with them all*. See that no one repays anyone evil for evil, but always seek to do good to one another and to everyone. (1 Thess. 5:14–15)

"Make sure it is the idle and not the fainthearted whom you admonish. Be clear it is the fainthearted and not the idle whom you are encouraging," Paul says. And then Paul reveals what this congregational work of discernment and care will require. "Whether a person is idle, fainthearted, or in need of help, whether you are admonishing someone or encouraging her, be certain of this," Paul said. "Be patient with them all."

But how do we show patience in the midst of mean accusation or mischaracterizations? Paul answered. Even when someone does them evil, he exhorts them to wait out their legitimate emotions rather than spew them. They are to bear with their deep wound.

In our day, that would equate to waiting two or three days before responding to the e-mail and holding back the fury in an immediate voice mail. They (and we) are to find perspective and healing from a source other than the temporary gratification from rushing to repay the evil done to them. They are to wait out their racing thoughts and emotions until they can choose good, even for an enemy. Then this wrestling toward praise, prayer, and gratitude without ceasing for every circumstance they face, and seeking in it what is from God's Spirit (and letting go of what is not)—this reveals the pathway patience takes (1 Thess. 5:16–22).

> The Lord's servant must not be quarrelsome but kind to everyone, able to teach, *patiently enduring evil,* correcting his opponents with gentleness. (2 Tim. 2:24–25)

Resisting the illusory desire for immediate defense, immediate remedy, and immediate relief is not easy pastorally. A patient gentleness requires courage and strength. For example, an e-mail is seductive bait for a quarrel. I noticed that I had not seen a dear family at church for a while. I contacted the family to inquire about how they were doing. I received an e-mail from the man in response. I hadn't seen the family because they had left our church. The e-mail reads like this:

> In short, despite the many good experiences we had at Riverside, and the people we really appreciated, we decided to try to find a church more suited to what we realized we need. Basically, we are looking for a church where the gospel is presented a lot; where doctrine is embraced and taught, where whole passages of the Bible are presented each Sunday. I don't fault Riverside for being the church that it is. It is a church going in the same direction that a LOT of American churches seem to be going. I trust that it is very effective for many people.
>
> Just so you know, we haven't found anywhere that fits us yet. It's getting very frustrating, and we have even considered (shudder!) trying to start a small home-church. I feel totally unequipped to do that. The thing is, though, I know several others (men in particular, and none from Riverside) who are equally frustrated with the modern American church and who have all talked about starting one ourselves. Not that we have the time, and of course none of us are preachers.

An e-mail like this—especially during a week or a season of multiple critiques—challenges us. Hearing that one does not present the gospel a lot, teach doctrine, or highlight the Bible, and that along with most churches we have more of sociology and therapy than we do the gospel, is tough. It can feel like a punch in the stomach that knocks the wind out, particularly when we know ourselves to pursue the gospel overtly and biblically in all we are attempting to do. Such criticism is made even more difficult when, in the context of friendship, the sender never mentions such things.

In addition, flaws or intentions to grow are given no room. When perfection to the desired standard isn't met, a person leaves rather than joining in to help. Finally, to slip away without conversation and isolate oneself is disconcerting to a pastor. We are tempted to take this as a personal statement about our identity. But my rushing to defend, to (un)kindly instruct, or to try to immediately fix is likely unwise and will prove unhelpful. A waiting of some kind will be required. Sometimes the waiting will last. No resolution will come until Jesus does.

All this having to wait during the invisible of the week can also seep into our preaching if we are not careful.

> Preach the word; be ready in season and out of season; reprove, rebuke, and exhort, *with complete patience* and teaching. (2 Tim. 4:2)

We have to resist the naïve or manipulative assumption that just because we preached or said something to someone once, they should hereafter immediately, always, and forever get it right. That's impatient preaching. Impatient preaching enables the listener to avoid wrestling with a question; it expects the listener to always ask, feel, or think the right way immediately; it presumes that growing in Jesus does not require days, weeks, months, and years.

What Paul teaches pastors about their work of patience, Jesus also taught. Those who make it through devilish assaults (Luke 8:11–12), the trials of the world (Luke 8:13), and misguided desires of the flesh (Luke 8:14) will require patience in Jesus to do so.

> As for that in the good soil, they are those who, hearing the word, hold it fast in an honest and good heart, and *bear fruit with patience.* (Luke 8:15)

We Will Have to Help Each Other

I had no ability to do this or be this. I needed help, and the help came.

A hurricane has an eye within its center where the calm dwells. Amid the worst moments of our swirling windstorms at our church, it slowly became apparent to me that in the center of it all, our core families and leaders were holding firm. Their friends were leaving. But they were not. I was not the only one holding on trying to gain stamina for a race I didn't want to run. So were they. Absent this core commitment to go the distance together, we would not have made it. When the storm hits, it helps to assess who is in the eye of it all and around what they are united. In this case, it was our common hope of what Jesus could still do in our church for this community.

After my black plague of an Easter sermon, Joe asked me if we could have lunch. We talked about our families, each other, Jesus, our church. At the end he said something small but huge: "Zack, I respect who you are as a man, a dad, and our pastor. I'm in this with you. We are doing this together. I've noticed a small thing, and I wonder if you'd give some time to think about it."

"Yes," I said. "Anything. Of course."

"You know how in music you have major chords and minor chords?"

I nodded.

"Lately, I've noticed that you've been emphasizing the minor chords in your preaching. Don't get me wrong. We need grace in the minor chords. I don't know how I'd even be standing right now if I was you. You inspire me. But maybe there is a major chord or two that you could play more often than you currently are. I think that might help you and help us too. Would you mind thinking about that?"

I did think about that. This elder gave me grace words of commitment and help. While many stormed about, windblown and frantic regarding the sermon and other things, he just spoke to me from the eye of it all. I'll never forget it.

What Paul said about Titus comes to mind: "Our bodies had no rest, but we were afflicted at every turn—fighting without and fear within. But God, who comforts the downcast, comforted us by the coming of Titus" (2 Cor. 7:5–6).

Paul and his team felt bodily fatigue, internal fear, and external conflict in a local place. The comfort came in the smallest, almost overlooked way, mainly by spending bits of time with a friend. We the downcast can no longer afford to enter these marathons alone.

In fact, when I think back about all that we had seen in my first four years, I became most amazed by the strength of this church's core group. They had had four leadership changes in six years. They left the stability of a larger, established church for the discomfort of believing that Jesus would empower a new gospel effort in this part of town for his glory. They were still here, waiting. How could that be? I began to think to myself, *What if they were the truly honorable ones? What if their faith amid these days of small things revealed that they were the true spiritual success stories in our community?*

I admired and learned from the patience of this core group. I have needed to learn patience with those who drifted. And all of us have required patience with me. I had tasted a kind of betrayal, including the sting of evangelicals who aren't at their best when they smell a scandal on you. I'd been scared of people, particularly church people, in a way that was uncomfortably new. The emotional abrasions from such a massive critique of my life and ministry had led me twice to offer my resignation. Early on, the constant vulnerability as a single dad seemed too much. My eventual dating and remarriage as a pastor in the public eye was sometimes cruel. But these elders, they kept saying that they believed God was at work. "Be patient," they'd say. "Hang on."

One night I shared my fears with my elders. Tears and fears flowed embarrassingly free. "Zack," Ty said, "if the worst ever happened, and this church we love folded, we will be standing here with you, the last to turn out the lights. We are with you and hope you will be with us even if it comes to that."

There is a strange sweetness that can be found amid the answer-less ache of an impending threat, going for days without what you know would be easier if you just had it already answered in your hands. Patience says to your empty hands, "God is here." Patience looks the worst in the face and says, "God will not leave you."

Patience Takes Time

I am trying to say that God speaks this "unleaving" to us in the smallest, almost overlooked ways. Often in Titus-like presence and sentences, these are the gifts sent from God, whispering amid the rattle and clang.

I was sitting with my pastor friend at a local coffee shop that I frequent in Webster Groves. He is a Kiwi—meaning that he is from New Zealand. I am a Hoosier—meaning that I'm from Indiana (except here in Missouri where the word *Hoosier* means something akin to good-for-nothing).

I sipped my coffee and began to pile on the self-pity as I connected dot after dot of discouraging themes. In time I would need to resist and undo this negative dot connecting. I also would need to lead our congregation through its own need to do the same, to finally come out from underneath old and fading narratives that no longer accounted for who we were becoming and the good work that God had done among us. But that would all come later.

For now, my Kiwi friend simply listened kindly and quietly as I spiraled down into self-absorption, pain, and complaint. He is a man who pastors in places where gospel churches are sometimes so few that there isn't a church down the street for pastors or congre-gants to go to instead. Sometimes pastors must work other jobs just to pay the rent. Inhabiting that context, he shows a kind and wise restraint toward my large, notable, and now assumptions regarding all that I imagine should have happened by now.

"Zack," he risked. "You know your belief in doing small things slowly over a long while?"

"Yes," I nodded.

Then he paused. "That's going to take some time," he said.

I stared at him.

We lingered.

He began to grin.

The truth of his words began to sink in.

I sat back in my chair and shook my head. I took a deep breath and then began to half-laugh at the thought. He began to laugh too.

Laughter and grace soon found each other.

Patience requires patience.

Going a long distance takes more time than speed.

Sometimes we need an ordinary friend in an overlooked moment of unanswered hurries to remind us.

PART THREE

Reshaping Our Inner Life

9

A New Ambition

Every man has a man within him who must die.

CHRISTIAN WIMAN

There once was a man who cared so much about trees that he traveled constantly on their behalf. But while he educated everywhere and tended personally to infected arbors far and wide, storms and swarms came through the man's hometown from time to time. Gusts blew down the pine and oak in his neighborhood. Their local roots, it turns out, had hollowed and weakened with rot. While he was busy and respected dispensing wisdom for bark and leaf, trees were falling in the man's own yard. No one was there to tend them.

Detox

When Jesus begins to rescue us from trying to fix it all, know it all, be everywhere for all as fast and as famously as possible, we find ourselves in a hard spot. We often enter what old-timers called "the dark night of the soul."[1] We have to come home to tend our own roots. The absence of movement unsettles us. A kind of spiritual detox sets in. We become like smokers trying to quit. We grumble and pace in search of gum to chew or worse.

Up till now, for example, if you've been everywhere for all, you have gotten through each day by utilizing technological screens, social media, e-mails, and phones and by attending another meeting, another cause, or another schedule, again. Envy, covetousness, and self-promotion have lurked here. Many people have applauded you for always coming through for them. But you've also caused people to feel stuck by your clingy presence, arrogant by your constant self-promotion, or untrusted if they tried to do something without you. Those at home have felt you hold them back or leave them abandoned by your always need to be somewhere other than where you are and who you are with. Your dark and growing need to be needed has become more apparent to them than to you.

If you've been a know-it-all, up till now you've habitually gotten through the day by relying on news, headlines, blogs, books, words, theologies, commentaries, conferences, videos, libraries, talk shows, conversations, or study hall. Being in the know among the answers and the answerers is what you've used to get through a day and make ministry work. Gossip, slander, and arrogance have lurked here too. People have loved it and praised you for the way you've kept the world answered, clean, and straight for them. But others have begun to feel more used than known by you. They've learned that you are not to be disagreed with. Somewhere along the line they have just stopped trying to contribute their thoughts. You have lost the ability to stay silent while someone else has a thought. Even if they agree with you, it's hard to imagine letting them move on without making sure that they take your thoughts with them.

Tempted to fix it all, you've been accustomed to feverishly reacting, impatient to find something, anything, that would constantly stop what discomforts people or you. You've gotten through each day by strong emotion or manipulative passivity with speed and flurry along with a constant re-creation of programs, slogans, signs, words, personnel, and even chair arrangements to solve troubles. People have loved the way you've always kept them moving with the steps they've needed to resist discomfort. But impatience has lurked here too. You have begun to use unmeditated anger, fear, sadness, or interruption. People have begun to feel emotionally frenzied, steamrolled, not busy enough, and unable to do enough to make things good enough for you. Even if they are emotionally fine, you can't fully believe them. You've lost your ability to handle a negative emotion and have begun to find solutions when no problems exist. Made for a crisis, you don't know what to do in a time of peace because you yourself are little acquainted with peace and quiet. Eventually people have begun to keep what troubles them to themselves.

Not only have you faithfully passed on the good content of the gospel, but you realize now that you've also passed on these misguided attempts to be like God. In Christ, you know it's time to let this whole apparatus go. But it's 2:15 p.m. on Wednesday afternoon. Things feel worse before they get better. For the next sixty minutes nothing on this list is going to help you, and you feel the discomfort of health.

> Look at a screen (TV, computer, phone, tablet, device); check social media; check e-mail; buy anything; make a phone call; check your schedule; meet with anybody other than your spouse or kids; attend a meeting; check the news; read a book; check a blog post; go to the library; go to a coffee shop; listen to a podcast; prepare a sermon; prepare a Bible study; play a game; use an app; create a ministry program; evaluate a program; tinker with the vision statement; make a brochure; move furniture; change the logo or signs; check the budget; put your anger or fear or sadness on somebody; say the first thing that comes to mind; express the first emotion you feel; eat or drink or speak to people; search for news.

If you can't do any of these things for the next sixty minutes, what is left to do? It's not that such things are bad. We've already established their help. But when they've become the starters on our team rather than support from the bench, we've lost sight of the game we've been called to play. Take away these crutches, and we have to learn to walk again. But how? We first have to return to a God-centered life.

Interrupting God

My children are fond of a knock-knock joke about an interrupting cow. In the joke the cow always says "moo" just when the other person starts to speak. The cow is impatient. He cannot wait. He interrupts with the right voice at the wrong time so that what the other person would say is never heard.

You and I have to confess that we know-it-alls, fix-it-alls, and everywhere-for-alls are the interrupting cow. But our interruptions aren't a joke. By all our ministry activity to mistakenly be like God, we've actually made it hard for people to see or hear him. Calvin made this plain. It startled me the first time I read it:

> We do not calmly hear God speaking to us, when we seem to ourselves to be very wise, but by our haste interrupt him when addressing us. . . . And, doubtless, no one can be a true disciple of God, except he hears him in silence. He does not, however, require the silence of the Pythagorean school, so that it should not be right to inquire whenever we desire to learn what is necessary to be known; but he would only have us to correct and restrain our forwardness, that we may not, as it commonly happens, unseasonably interrupt God, and that as long as he opens his sacred mouth, we may open to him our hearts and our ears, and not prevent him to speak.[2]

For all our sermons, Bible studies, vision statements, lunches, meetings, tweets, podcasts, and church management sessions, we constantly hear our own voice. So do others. For many of us, it has been a long while since we've heard God in the quiet, knowing that it was his voice and not ours. We stare into our detox and begin to realize that we have been like a rude spokesperson in the presence of our host. Etiquette requires that our host offer welcome and invitation to everyone. Only then does the host alert all present of his spokesman who can answer any questions or tend to their needs that evening on his behalf. The spokesman speaks only after the host has spoken and only then for the sake of upholding what the host desires. Imagine what it would be like for us as a guest if the spokesman kept trying to speak first or kept interrupting what the host was saying to us? I'm trying to say that I never imagined that by my fix-it, know-it, everywhere-famous-and-speedily ministry of the Word, I could actually, as Calvin says, "interrupt God" as he addresses those he has called me to serve on his behalf or as he is trying to address me. There is "a time to speak," yes, but also, "a time to keep silence" (Eccles. 3:7). To let this apparatus go you must become acquainted with the silence warranted when in the presence of the living God.

Silences, Not Just Sentences

When I first began pastoral work, the formative texts were "Preach the word" (2 Tim. 4:2) and "Do the work of an evangelist" (2 Tim. 4:5). Over the years I have written extensively and attempted earnestly to uphold these essential aspects of pastoral work.[3]

But I've also come to believe that we pastors are prone "toward too many words."[4] I'm not speaking about sermon length. Short sermons say nothing necessarily about the condition of a pastor's inner life. I'm referring to how we as pastors use words to manage our families or ministries or to preserve us from having vulnerably to face what we cannot control. Along the way, therefore, a wisdom text has joined these others to inform my daily pastoral work. "Know this, my beloved brothers: let every person be quick to hear, slow to speak, slow to anger" (James 1:19).

To be quick to listen means that we do not say the first thing or everything we think (slow to speak), even if we are right, even if we are preachers or evangelists. Nor do we give immediate voice or vent even to the strongest emotions that pulsate within our chests (slow to anger), no matter how strongly we feel them.

If you don't mind, take a moment and reread those last two sentences.

When James says, "every person," he includes those of us who preach and teach. Later he makes this connection even clearer. He cautions that "not many of [us] should become teachers," because we will face stricter judgment. Then James identifies our ability to stumble as cause for being cautious to teach (James 3:1). James then rolls out metaphor after metaphor to describe the danger of talk (James 3:2–12). His point is plain. Talk is hazardous. Teachers are talkers. Great care must therefore be taken. The wise must learn to "hear" (Prov. 1:5) before they speak.

Jesus possesses such wisdom. He leads us into an apprenticeship of secondary speaking. We speak as those who have first listened. Ours is not the first word on the scene.

> For I have not spoken on my own authority, but the Father who sent me has himself given me a commandment—what to say and what to speak. . . . What I say, therefore, I say as the Father has told me. (John 12:49–50)

Jesus's quiet is no manipulative silent treatment. It isn't an excuse for passive neglect. Nor is his quiet a ruse to avoid words altogether while silently judging us. "Simply to refrain from talking, without a heart listening to God, is not silence" in this wisdom sense.[5] Instead, Jesus shows us that he waits in silence for the Father's voice. Then he speaks.

"Silence means nothing other than waiting for God's Word."[6] We are silent early in the morning because God should have the first word, and we are silent before going to bed because the last word also belongs to God.[7] We grow more quiet before we speak throughout the day, as if moment by moment, scene by scene, we are waiting upon another in whose presence we propose to talk. What but this waiting upon God in the presence of others is our joy and task? Pastoral work such as corporate worship (Eccles. 5:1–3) and prayer (Matt. 6:7) aren't a forum to multiply our words and hear ourselves talk. We talk only as those listening for the voice of another. Jesus hasn't left us. In him we find mending grace to say of his voice what the poet said of the owl:

An owl sound wandered along the road with me.
I didn't hear it—I breathed it into my ears.[8]

Mark this down if you can. Silences, not just sentences, form the work of pastoral ministry. Wise pastors are listening preachers.

Ambition for the Quiet

When Jesus asks, "What do you want me to do for you?" we start over in our detox. We learn to say, "Please grant me a new ambition for a quiet life." Immediately I hear myself complain. "A quiet life can make no difference! If I don't talk and make things happen, how will I effect change? If I let my voice go unheard, how will my voice ever be heard? If I don't speak, I will be misunderstood. If I don't keep things going, who will? Quiet seems ordinary and passive. What about the work of God?"

Sage mentors ask us to pause here. They tell us to listen to what our thoughts are saying. They teach us that our complaint about quiet might expose foul ambitions lurking within. Old Matthew Henry says it this way:

> We must study to be quiet. . . . The most of men are ambitious of the honour of great business, and power, and preferment; they covet it, they court it, they compass sea and land to obtain it; but the ambition of a Christian should be carried out towards quietness.[9]

Henry establishes this new ambition in Paul's own words: "Aspire to live quietly, and to mind your own affairs" (1 Thess. 4:11). To study to be quiet refers to a willingness to be overlooked "out there" and to forgo what the world desires so as to be faithful to God with the portion given.

But how can we find a stamina for being overlooked in the world unless quiet also describes a Sabbath of the heart moment by moment with God?[10] A Sabbath heart describes an inner life pursuing rest in him. We don't fear the loss of worldly attention only because we enjoy company with true treasure. His attention is enough. His holding all things together is our trust. We believe this is true for anyone we would serve. This inner rest is part of what we help them cultivate.

But why? Because quiet like this pays off. When circumstances assail us, we study quiet of soul so that we can stay steady "in the midst of the greatest provocations"[11] and "unevennesses of Providence."[12] When people storm at us with their inability to listen and their insistence to say everything they think and feel, we rest more solidly on this fact: "A needful truth spoken in a heat, may do more hurt than good, and offend rather than satisfy."[13] We weather the storm and wait to react, if at all, after the winds have died down.

I hear the objections grumble within me again. "But Paul writes those words for a particular context of Christians who struggled to care for their local place with actual work. Paul didn't mean what Henry said, that *all Christians* must make quiet their study and ambition. Certainly he didn't mean that pastors should do so. Pastors shouldn't grow ambitious for a quiet life! They are supposed to make a difference!"

Henry's words come back to me, and I ask myself, "If we as pastors aren't supposed to study to be quiet, does that mean that contrary to other Christians, our task is to study to be noisy? Are we meant to urge others to this kind of inner rest amid the provocations of life when we ourselves don't possess it? And in this grumbling aren't you forgetting, Zack, that beneath your vocation as a pastor you are an ordinary Christian who needs your heart at rest with God—not for the sake of your ministry, but for the sake of your own life?"

What is more, Henry doesn't identify quiet with a tone of voice or a day among the lilies for repose. As meaningful as those things can be, Henry connects inner rest with our conscience. "We are accustomed to say, 'We will give any thing for a quiet life.'—I say, anything for a quiet conscience."[14]

Isn't conscience our agitator? It shouts at us, and we fever about to know, fix, and be as fast as possible to get the most affirmation necessary to assure our inner being or those we serve that we are enough and that our ministry is good. We bustle about trying to be like God because we don't yet sensibly feel that it is okay and fitting not to be.

Perhaps we now feel unnerved. In Ecclesiastes 9:17, the word "quiet" carries the idea of trust or contented rest.[15] The first time you try to go a whole day with no access to anything but God at a local retreat center, you begin to fuss into frustration. Lingering among silences makes us feel like toddlers entering the nursery on Sunday mornings. When our parent drops us off, we feel abandoned. We either tantrum about, or we cling to anything or anyone that promises to hold us.

Charles Spurgeon, the old Baptist preacher, explains why. "Quietude, some men cannot abide," he says, "because it reveals their inner poverty." Take away the crutches we use to hold up our fix-it, know-it, and be-everywhere personas, and the broken legs of our intimacy with God buckle. "Priceless as the gift of utterance may be," he says, "the practice of silence in some aspects far excels it." He adds:

> I am persuaded that most of us think too much of speech, which after all is but the shell of thought. Quiet contemplation, still worship, unuttered rapture . . . rob not your heart of the deep sea joys; miss not the far-down life, by for ever babbling among the broken shells and foaming surges of the shore.[16]

Quiet is a means of God's grace. Within it, God shows us our inner poverty and misguided ambitions. He has waited patiently with a quiet heart while we've brewed our lives into storm and froth constantly interrupting him. Now that we are finally silent, he has healing to speak, mending to perform. We have held on to fixing, knowing, and being everywhere as fast and as famous as we can, like a toddler who can't go a day without his blankie. But there comes a time when the toddler must age into wisdom and learn to sleep without it. The first night and day of trying this are detox ugly. But soon, the rest comes and the freedom blesses all in the house.

A Pastor's Provocations

In this regard, two old pastors and one younger give three pieces of good advice in our detox. I know well that each of these older pastors was imperfect; also, that they may represent traditions with which you disagree. But being an imperfect or even a profoundly mistaken pastor is no sign of having nothing right or good in Christ to say to us. I find this out every time I preach. So stay listening if you can. Wise help lingers here.

1) The boundaries of your calling reveal
God's pastoral care for you.

John Calvin wants us to know that in order to protect us from turning our lives upside down with anxieties, strivings, misguided cravings, heavings, and rash collisions, "each individual has his own kind of living assigned to him by the Lord as a sort of sentry post so that he may not heedlessly wander about throughout life."[17]

It's Wednesday at 2:00 p.m. You try to be quiet. But when you do, you imagine someone else's calling and wish that you had it. You try to cross over the boundaries of your responsibilities and gather up theirs for yourself too. Quiet can't be found here. Not for long. Let go. Trust God's peace for you. It is "no slight relief from cares, labors, troubles, and other burdens for a man to know that God" has given him this particular sentry post for this time. By freeing you from trying to do something he hasn't asked you to do, he intends you to experience his contented "consolation." Knowing that this post is given you by him enables you to "bear and swallow discomforts, vexations, weariness, and anxieties in his way of life," for you are at least "persuaded that the burden was laid" upon you "by God."[18]

In other words, even the pastoral vocation is itself God's pastoral care for those he calls to it. So here I sit in my study. It is

Monday morning in Webster Groves. Skies grey with frosty rain, the week begins cold. Contrary to what doing something else and grand imagines for me, Jesus is here too with his coat on. He was awake before I was. He has work to do in this Missouri town. For his purposes, he called me, and not you, to enter this joyful and tear-making work with him. If he made this call, the work must matter to him. If I'm the one for it, there must be a wise reason. This means that I have mattering work to do even if in my whole life I never get to do your work—the mattering work you get to do out there that I sometimes restlessly and naïvely imagine would make me happier or more significant. Please forgive me. I have prayers to say for persons you've never heard of. I'd best get on with this good work of the day. You'd best get on with yours too.

2) In trying so hard not to miss out, you actually create the thing you fear.

John Cassian describes ministers restless not only for the callings of others but also for their gifts. "They hear people talked about because of zeal or virtue other than their own."[19] Anything another minister does well becomes an occasion, not for our gratitude to God for the sake of the other minister and the cause of the gospel in our generation, but a reason for us to wring our hands and pressure ourselves because now we too must equal or better what that other minister can do. If we can't do what everyone else can do all the time, we believe that somehow we are poor ministers. When you try to hold on to gifts that God did not give to you, you lose quiet and increase your "spiritual turmoil" as you restlessly desire "to take up pursuits different from" your own. But this disquiet is "deadly danger." After all, "it sometimes happens that what some do quite rightly others mistakenly imitate."[20]

Therefore remember, "it is quite impossible for one and the same man to shine outstandingly" in all the gifts listed by Paul. "If one tries to pursue them all together what happens of necessity is that in chasing them all, one does not really catch any of them, and out of this changing about and variety, one draws loss rather than gain."[21] In other words, we miss out on every pleasant thing God already had for us. We don't see such delights because they are right in front of us.

3) Smaller is always better than larger unless, and only if, God extrudes us.

We lose rest of soul when we believe that bigger is better. The Serpent tempts all of us to believe that some places matter more than others, that some people matter more than others, and that our strategies and gifts rather than God's wise calling are our answer.

But in Luke 14:7–11, Jesus teaches those who follow him to seek the lowest, not the highest, seats at the table. Francis Schaeffer points out how many of us pastors believe the opposite of what Jesus teaches. In our way of thinking, "we are tempted to say, 'I will take the larger place because it will give me more influence for Jesus Christ.'" But Jesus teaches us that we should determine to take the lower place unless the Lord himself "extrudes us" into the larger one.[22]

We are tempted to take up something "big" in our eyes or in the eyes of others for his name and lose sight of him altogether. Not only does the smaller place enable us humbly and gratefully to have a seat at the table; it enables us daily to sit in his presence, eating his food, hearing his words, delighting in him. Who would ever want to leave this seat? Many of us take larger roles without having the strength yet to disappoint the important people who wait for us there. After all, if we go to the larger place, we will do so by slowing them down so that we and they can still listen to God. Take the smaller seat then, the seat that allows you such presence with Jesus, instead of the large seat that would take this quiet from you. Only go if the one who calls is going there with you. Only go if you are ready to remain committed there, regardless of size, to the small, mostly overlooked mattering things in Jesus.

Most of us have no category for what I just said. For the bulk of my pastoral ministry, neither have I. We need help, and the help comes. Pastors need the poor wise man.

Forgotten Deliverers

In Ecclesiastes 9 we are told the story of a poor wise man who once delivered a small place with a small population from violent siege by an arrogant king. The king and his besieging army saw the man's poverty, considered him irrelevant, and mistakenly paid no more attention to him. But this powerful king underestimated wisdom. He was outwitted by the poor wise man and left in defeat. The small group of people and their little place in the world were rescued!

What do you suppose happened next? I envision a rags-to-riches story in which the poor wise man who delivered the city becomes celebrated. But in this biblical story, what many of us fear most actually happened. The city forgot all about him. This was no platform for greater relevance. Needless to say, this was not a pastoral theology text for me early on. Can you blame me? Notice the obituary.

All his life, he lived with very little in a small place among a small number of people doing a good that no one remembered.

But notice what God says about this poor wise man and his overlooked life of victories: "The words of the wise heard in quiet are better than the shouting of a ruler among fools" (Eccles. 9:17). Read that again, won't you?

The ruler, like folly, was loud. He made much of his fame (great), position (king), visible resources (building great siegeworks), power (might), and followers (he besieged the city) (Eccles. 9:14).

In contrast, the man who heard in quiet, the man of God, was poor. A man who is poor has only his humbled self to offer. There is no noise to his appearance. In this case his poverty was physical, not emotional or mental. His lack had to do with materials and appearances, not substance or grace.

Pastoral work requires presence. But whether we are introverted or extroverted, rural or urban, in large churches or small, our temptation to resist humbled presence remains the same. We are mistakenly prone to follow the great ruler in this wisdom story rather than the poor wise man. We present ourselves as the fixer, the knower, the one who is everywhere and quick to heal. But the sage of Ecclesiastes redirects us. The poor wise man's poverty means that we cannot use him for his money, his status, his political position, his power, his accomplishments, or who he might know in order to help us make connections and network with others. There is nothing this man can offer us in the world but his testimony of God, the integrity of his way, and the grace in his life. These two differing ways of being represent two contrasting powers for our trust—the power of folly versus the power of wisdom. Wisdom is found in the humbled presence of the poor man. So, then, is the power of God.

I now find myself asking God on Sunday mornings, "Lord, please deliver me from praying and preaching in some kind of preacher voice today. Rescue me to pray and preach with the voice you hear in the night watches or in the day when I cry to you and no one else is around."

I am also asking God to deliver me from thinking that I must offer folly by my presence in order to be successful in gospel ministry. I am asking for the stamina to be overlooked even in the church by those who weren't seeking what was humbly wise to begin with. I am asking because I have no way of doing any of this myself. But Jesus does. Though he was "one from whom men hide their faces," he was bearing our griefs, carrying our sorrows, being wounded for our transgressions, and crushed for our iniquities. From our foolish vantage point we "esteemed him stricken, smitten by God, and afflicted," and we looked elsewhere for rescue. But the chastisement that brought us peace was actually upon him the whole time, and by his stripes we are healed—even those of us like sheep who turned away (Isa. 53:3–6)! Jesus is the poor wise man after all, isn't he? The poor wise man who delivered those who forgot him. He has rescued our city in the quiet and calls us to relevance of a different kind.

Solitude, Hospitable Presence, Wisdom

When we constantly interrupt what God is saying to our hearts, we interrupt solitude—our sense that in our aloneness with God we are not lonely but with him truly as we are and as he is. Solitude waits for his word and lead. It enables us to tend to all that swirls within us and to discern the difference between his voice and ours, his voice and the voices all around us, so that we respond to him rather than react to our first-draft thought and emotion. Solitude of heart with God graciously transitions us from reacting to responding.

Additionally, when we constantly interrupt what God is saying to those around us, we interrupt hospitality. By "hospitality" I do not refer to setting the table and placing food upon it. I refer instead to what that picture indicates. We are capable of welcoming other human beings just as they are, even when they believe or say, look or smell, other than we want them to. Hospitality graciously transitions us from consuming people to welcoming them without fixing, knowing, and being for them what only God can.

When we constantly interrupt God's timing in the circumstances that we and others face, we interrupt wisdom. Wisdom is "the fear of the LORD" (Prov. 9:10), the recognition that God has preceded us every moment and his voice about that moment is true. His timing, which values smaller, mostly overlooked mattering things, is not always efficient or large or immediate.

In all our attempts to do for God without waiting for him, we've lost our quiet heart, our capacity for treating neighbors with hospitable room rather than using them for our platform or strategic plan, and we lose our ability to wait with discernment for God's timing and ways. We've grown reactive, consuming of others, and hasty, and all of this for God. This means that we are likely to mentor others into these qualities as well.

With Jesus, Alone with the Father

I mean none of this tritely. I am a man of anxiety. Bouts of panic or depression are mine to own. Add to this my ambitions, which are restless for anything but quiet with God. They haunt my soul and find misguided applause everywhere I look. Make no mistake. A quiet heart is grace given and fought for with our Lord. Pray with me, won't you? Here in the detox, resistant to what it means finally to be still, remember your Savior. He knows what it is to be overlooked, emptied, even painfully alone. But he tells us that he is not alone. Even in the desolate place the Father keeps company with him (John 16:32). Therefore, let the old pastor Richard Baxter recount this promise of solitude for you too. In Christ, no matter how much noise and clang we've sinfully pined for, we too, right now, can say by grace, "I am not alone because the Father is with me."[23]

Then let Baxter stir your faith into declaration. Perhaps you feel the terrible discomfort of health. Let me say kind words to you. This moment, if you find yourself in a wilderness rather than in your preferred city, in a prison rather than in a palace, know this: when you are with the Father, you can say, without being trite or naïve, "Let that wilderness be my city, and that prison my palace as long as I abide on earth." As long as I have this company with God, "it is no disadvantage," even "if by mortal eyes I am seen no more."[24]

Therefore, while loud kings ruckus about and crowds cheer, relevance speaks humbly in the desolate place. In the quiet God is heard and the mending begins.

10

Beholding God

God is a delicious good.

THOMAS WATSON

Quiet with God in the presence of our aloneness, we grow in solitude of heart.

Quiet with God in the presence of people, we offer hospitable welcome.

Quiet with God in the presence of our circumstances, we offer everyone a chance at wisdom.

A Different Purpose

But when we make the study of quiet our ambition, and we propose to become listening preachers among the mattering things, it poses a severe problem to our ministry approach. If our purpose as pastors is to do large things, famously, as fast as possible so that everyone is mobilized to do great things by fixing everything, knowing it all, and being everywhere for God, this purpose and quiet are at odds.

I've needed to see how the study of quiet and the pastoral vocation work together. I've found help in Isaiah 50. I'll highlight verse 4:

The Lord GOD has given me
>   the tongue of those who are taught,
that I may know how to sustain with a word
>   him who is weary.
Morning by morning he awakens;
>   he awakens my ear
>   to hear as those who are taught.

Our theme from the last chapter returns. God takes the initiative. He wakes us day by day. He teaches us in solitude to talk to others as those who have been taught. We talk as those who are listening for God daily. But why does this suffering servant waken and listen in morning rhythm to God's initiative? He tells us plainly: "That I may know how to sustain with a word him who is weary."

The weary ones are at their end. No resources remain that can uphold them. What do such "weary" and "exhausted" people need? To know that there is one who "gives power to the faint, and to him who has no might he increases strength. . . . They who wait for the LORD shall renew their strength; they shall mount up with wings like eagles; they shall run and not be weary; they shall walk and not faint" (Isa. 40:28–31).

Jesus fulfills and takes up this listening talk. As the suffering servant, he learned daily from the Father how to do this, and he did (Matt. 11:28–30). Hospitable presence (sustaining him who is weary) is made possible by solitude of heart with God (morning by morning he wakens me).

The apostle Paul learned from Jesus this same purpose and skill of grace. "Let your speech always be gracious, seasoned with salt," Paul said. But why? "So that you may know how you ought to answer each person" (Col. 4:6). We speak what "is good for building up, as fits the occasion." Why? "That it may give grace to those who hear" (Eph. 4:29).

When Jesus asks, "What do you want me to do for you?" we've put listening preacher on our bucket list. We've asked to study quiet. Now we add, "O Lord, grant that by the end of my days, I will have learned from you how to sustain with a word him who is weary." The purpose of quiet with God is hospitable welcome to the weary.

For all of Jesus's use of silences and sentences, he never breaks a bruised reed; he never snuffs out a flickering wick (Isa. 42:3). In my cravings to do something great for God I would not have identified this purpose as my own. This purpose sounds too small. It is like saying that I want to be a pastor because my great ambition in life is to learn how to help an ordinary person in his or her struggle to locate God. I laugh with regret and shake my head. Tell me: when did it happen that a life purposed to help ordinary people in their ordinary struggles locate God became too small a thing?

A Different Way to Learn

If we want to learn an ambition for quiet in order to hospitably sustain the weary, we need to adjust or expand our way of learning.

An ancient story describes a young man who entreated an old sage. "Please, master, be my teacher." From that moment the old sage invited the young man to accompany him wherever he went and in whatever he did. But after a while the young man grew impatient, for although the master welcomed many visitors and often gave them counsel, the old sage never spoke in this same way to the young man. Finally, the young man could bear this no more. He shouted, "Master, I have given away everything to follow you! Why won't you teach *me* like you teach *others*?"

The old sage listened with compassion and responded, "Do you not know that every moment you have spent with me has offered you my teaching? Everything I do and say, whether in public or private, is set before you plainly."

The young man remained frustrated and confused. After a moment, the old sage suddenly shouted, "Unlike my other students, what you receive from me, you receive directly!"

At that moment, the eyes of the young man's heart were opened.[1]

In history, one of Jesus's followers had a similar experience. Jesus told Philip and the others that they know God the Father and have seen him. Confused, Philip said to Jesus, "Lord, show us the Father, and it is enough for us."

Jesus responded. "Have I been with you so long, and you still do not know me, Philip? Whoever has seen me has seen the Father. How can you say, 'Show us the Father'?" (John 14:4–9).

It is as if Jesus says, in response: "What other of my words, works, and ways would you need for your learning that I have not already offered you by giving you intimate access to my daily life?"

It is almost as if Philip only knew to grow attentive to gathered crowds, public teaching, and direct words. In the shadows cast by larger and louder things, Philip could look right at the small, daily, mostly overlooked ways of Jesus and not know that he was meant to discern the Father in these too.

If you want to learn quiet, you have to learn to grow attentive to the implicit and boring graces thriving with life right in front of you. Listening preachers learn how to behold.

Learning How to Behold Again

The word *behold* is used numerous times in the Scriptures. To behold is to stop everything for a moment in order to fix our complete attention upon something. Meditatively, we linger with it so that from the quiet contemplation of it, we can discern God's relation to it and derive from him the meaning he sees in it.

Sages, like the poor wise man in our last chapter, were taught to behold God's creation and creatures, including the conditions of creation (Prov. 24:31), the ways of people in their sin (Prov. 7:10), the pains of people in being sinned against (Eccles. 4:1), and the interior workings of our hearts before God (Prov. 24:12).

This wisdom community also sought to behold God in his providence, including God's works in history (Ps. 46:8), the good provisions of God in ordinary life (Eccles. 5:18), the truth of something good as it is lived out in our experience (Ps. 133:1), the good presence of God on our behalf moment by moment (Ps. 33:18), and the moment-by-moment promise of God's present help (Ps. 54:4).[2]

Throughout the Gospels, Jesus regularly calls upon us to behold in these sage ways.

When we do, these dear ones who were blurry to us before because of how close, small, and ordinary they seemed, now come graciously into focus among the mattering things. To behold God in all things daily changes the way we learn and alters what we look at. We begin to listen and look at people and their lives in such a way that helps them locate the otherwise "unapparent presence of God."[3] Beholding leads us gradually to say by grace:

> Now the ears of my ears are awake
> Now the eyes of my eyes are opened.[4]

Pastoral work that is contemplative in this beholding way arranges and entertains all things from the vantage point of this fear of the Lord so as to reverently and gratefully contemplate God as the creator, ruler, sole healer, and only true interpreter of anything that we encounter, concerning everything that exists, anywhere that we are, at any time whatsoever.

In all of this, we are saying two basic things. (1) "The principal care and solicitude of our life [is] to seek God, to aspire to him with all the affection of our heart, and to repose nowhere else but in him alone";[5] and (2) people need your pastoral help locating God in their lives so that they can rest in him too.

Beholding Changes the Way We Meet with People

On crisis occasions, speed cannot be helped, but as a daily norm, beholding will lead you to schedule a pause in between meetings (and phone calls and e-mails) to listen and pray. What does this look like?

To begin, you confess that this meeting cannot fix it all, possess all knowledge, be everything for someone, or provide ultimate relief. It is Jesus who holds this meeting and all things together (Col. 1:17).

Next, you remember that God has preceded those of you who will meet. He is active with the persons you are about to meet (whether they realize it or not) long before they arrive in your study, and his activity toward them will continue after they leave. This tells us at least two things. (1) The others' meeting with God does not begin and end when you meet with them. (2) Consequently, you are not the most central or important part of this meeting. God is. God is allowing you to sit with others he has loved and pursued all the days of their lives.

So, before meetings now, I'm learning to ask God to "open doors" and for the grace to know what to say if anything needs being said (Col. 4:2–6). After the meeting, I'm learning to pause for prayer too. I know that devilish activity joins the cares and pains of the world to choke out anything good that was said (Matt. 13:19–22).

During the meeting itself there are now "pauses in between sentences and paragraphs," sometimes awkward ones. After all, since God has preceded us, I am not to take charge of this meeting, not at first, except to invite us into listening as we talk. Just as it is foolhardy for a paramedic to arrive on the scene without checking various signs before rushing headlong into prescriptive action, so the sage or contemplative suffering servant does not propose answers without having first listened, questioned, and meditated. We listen to words and pauses. We intend to let none of them fall to the ground.[6] Not yet anyway. We gather them all up, as it were, holding them up for the Lord, who is present. We ask him to sort it all out and make of it what he will.

Then, "I've heard you say this," I might say. "A moment ago, I also heard you express something else," I continue. I then ask a question as I hold up these two threads of sentences. I'm listening as much as they are now. "Have you noticed how these two sentences seem connected (or disconnected) somehow?" What do you suppose God might want to show you about himself in these things?"

As we grow attentive to such threads, a passage from God's Word or, secondarily, in support of God's Word; an analogy from God's creation; or a scene or story from God's providence might now come to mind. This does not mean that we have it right or solved. We don't know yet if this verse, analogy, or scene is the right one for this moment, whether born out of our own mistakenness or wonderfully illumined for us to light our path in Jesus by his Spirit.

Or perhaps a long awkward silence results from the question. I'm learning to resist the temptation to fill it. Instead, I begin internally to pray and wait. They find their words. I hear them. Now the sentences come more freely. He is the one we are seeking, after all. There in community together, anchored by his Word, listening in the silences, waiting, asking, seeking the present Christ, many times we experience the finding! Paul affirms that we should "seek God, and perhaps feel [our] way toward him and find him. Yet he is actually not far from each one of us" (Acts 17:27).

I'm not great at this, but recent comments spur me on not to quit. "I'm surprised by this meeting," he said to me. We had just spent an hour and fifteen minutes over lunch.

"You've never once looked at your watch," he continued. "I've been trying to speak my heart quickly. I figured you'd hurry me along or sit impatiently with me, needing to get on with your next meeting."

Then what he said next struck me. "I feel listened to like I'm a human being," he said. Then he paused and smiled. "I hardly ever feel that way, you know? Thank you so much."

Not every meeting can look like this. Sometimes crisis moments require emergency-room responses. And not everyone who has met with me can say what this man said. Taking time to settle prayerfully for the sake of pastorally listening to and beholding God while meeting another human being is not natural to me. But it is natural to the one we follow. As ambassador-discerners, we enter the stories of others and say, "Slow down. Look here, listen; God is showing you who he is." His wise words heard in the quiet deliver us both.

Beholding Changes the Way We Pray for Others

Making this kind of transition has been harder than I thought, but not because my calling to this kind of prayer and listening is unclear. "We will devote ourselves to prayer and to the ministry of the word" (Acts 6:4), the apostles plainly said. To devote oneself to something is to make that thing our business, the task around which everything else orbits. There is nothing unclear about that.

But early on I thought of this pastoral work of prayer and Word mostly in their visible and public forms. I imagined the public prayers I'd say on Sunday mornings in front of crowds gathered for worship (2 Tim. 2:1), or as Jesus did when he prayed in his public and priestly ways (John 17:1–26). I thought of ministry of the Word in terms of the sermons I would preach. I didn't realize then that a pastor's vocation with prayer and Word and care is many times invisible, tucked away with Jesus, in one-on-one or small-group moments hidden from the eyes of our congregation, attempting to behold God in the individual providences of an ordinary human being.

I therefore strongly underestimated where a vocation of prayer, Word, and entering the doubts and questions of another human being can take us. Beneath a plum tree or beside the rain-drenched graveside of a child; in a parking lot, or on a porch; in a bathroom of disability, or a courthouse of pain; in a hospital of unknowns or a bar. I didn't imagine an elevator, or a fireplace, in a banquet hall or on streets of riot and protest. Or standing beside cars with their busted windows, broken into by thieves and busted like the minds of those in the psych ward reaching for my hand. This is where beholding work takes us. He leads us into unknown-to-the-world places for the sake of unknown-to-the-world people so that we can know that God is with us, even us. Earnestly, then, in prayer, "we strive to descend in the depth of our heart and from there seek him, and not with the tongue or the throat only" but with our very hearts such as they are.[7]

We take this beholding work, done out there in the providences of those we serve, back with us to our study or office. We learn to seek God for those we serve even when we aren't with them. We contemplate how dear they are to God. Since the Bible itself is full of prayers,[8] perhaps we gather up these Scriptures and take out our church directory. While walking the empty sanctuary or outside in the neighborhood or in the quiet by a lit candle on a cold morning, we read a sentence from a prayer given in the Bible and then turn that sentence into praise and petition for the family or individual.

While we are doing this beholding work of prayer, the phone still rings, e-mails still arrive, demands don't quit, and almost all of them sound more urgent and more promising of my productivity than this. After all, "running the church" as important as it is can feel more productive and affirming than quiet beholding. But the feeling lies to us. Both kinds of work matter.

So we make our psalms to the Lord, not in an authoritative way for all God's people as King David did, but as a pupil in his school of prayer, crying out prayers in response to what confronts us each day.[9] This kind of psalm making can even feel like a mess sometimes.

A knock taps my study door. I get up from the floor. I've just been kneeling in prayer and leaning deep into my Papaw's chair, the one on which he held me when I was a boy. I grab a tissue, blow my nose, and open the door. "Hey! Come on in," I say. Then I add, "Don't mind me. I've just been crying, that's all."

"Oh," they say. "Are you okay? Should I come back later?"

I want to say yes. I'm scared to be known as I am. But by grace I'm learning to choose faith and say, "Oh, no worries. Some tears are worth crying, you know? Come on in. I've been eager to share time with you."

Such scenes are like a rare bird in my life—unusual to see but beautiful when sighted.

Beholding Changes the Way We Meet with God

Sometimes I light a candle. I lean against the wall in my study or sit in Papaw's worn leather chair. Maybe it's afternoon around 2 p.m. I read a Scripture promise—"He cares for you" (1 Pet. 5:7). I give thanks for what it says. I confide in the promise, which means I open up my heart to it. The Word of God is what lights my path.

It is my true candle. Then I say something like, "Here I am, Lord. You are my love, my delight. I want to know you and cast my cares upon you. I want to trust that you care for me and for those I love and serve."

Then I try to wait with no words for a moment in the presence of him who loves me and sees me in secret. But over the first several minutes my mind isn't silent. The thoughts and feelings that have gone unnoticed amid the chatter of the day seize their moment and rise loudly to the surface as I try to quiet down. The first round of these thoughts is like foam on a soda or cream on milk. We clear it away to get to what lies beneath. So, I take each thought that vies for my attention, no matter what it is, how silly or terrible, how ordinary or task oriented, how biblically inaccurate or theologically sound, and turn it into prayer, saying of each one, "I hear myself thinking this thing, Lord, and I bring it to you. I leave it with you."

By taking each thought to him, I am doing what Peter told me to, "casting all your anxieties on him, because he cares for you" (1 Pet. 5:7). Casting our cares is like reaching into a pile of mixed laundry, sorting out each cloth, and putting each piece back where it belongs. Or going through a worn garage of tools scattered everywhere. One by one I pick up each tool and hand it to God, and he puts it back where it belongs. As Calvin put it, this prayer is like "a communication between God and us whereby we expound to him our desires, our joys, our sighs, in a word, *all the thoughts of our hearts.*"[10]

Now the first blast of frothy thought has been cleared. It matters to know that often after the froth clearing and before the deep drinking in prayerful aloneness with God, boredom, restless mind, feelings of wasted time, and anxious fear all collaborate into a gang and try to loot us. They mosquito-bite us, and we want to get up, blow out the candle, and do anything but this.

Instead, I invite you to hold on (and I need you to invite me to do the same). Let's face our tantrumming or clinging souls in this detox deliberately. With Jesus's kindness and mercy set before us, we look again to the open book in candlelight; we let in the wise man's mentoring.

Imaginary Conversations

Beholding God in prayer offers us a kind of resistance to imaginary conversations too. Esau comforted and consoled himself with the thought of killing his brother Jacob (Gen. 27:42). He imagined the scene over and again, and the imaginary conversation provided misguided solace for his inner being.[11]

We know we are having an imaginary conversation when we hurt and talk to ourselves about someone else, using the second- rather than the third-person voice, as if these persons are actually standing there with us. Notice the psalmist begins to talk in God's presence as if the friend who has betrayed him is standing there. He shifts from third-person language (him) to second-person language (you):

> For it is not an enemy who taunts me—
> > then I could bear it;
> it is not an adversary who deals insolently with me—
> > then I could hide from him.
> But it is *you*, a man, my equal,
> > my companion, my familiar friend.
> *We* used to take sweet counsel together;
> > within God's house we walked in the throng.
> > > (Ps. 55:12–14)

What do we do when we find ourselves constantly talking to a person in imaginary ways rather than talking directly to God about our pain? We stop mid-sentence or we put a halt to the e-mail we are about to send. We turn instead to the present Lord and make our anxiety a real-time conversation with him. We may do this fifty times in a day. We may wait or not send that e-mail at all now. No matter. Jesus is with us apprenticing us to turn all our anxieties directly to the Father through him. This was his way too (Heb. 5:7).

Beholding Changes Our Definition of a Quiet Time

I suggest that our aloneness with God for an hour requires a metaphor change. A classroom-like quiet time has its place. We use it to gain more information from the Bible, and this is good. Without right information from the Bible our path has no light.

But solitude of heart in the desert wilderness reminds us that "it is written" was not a matter of mental information for Jesus but the source by which he held his identity intact. He went to the Father's words because the Devil discounted them. The Devil did not discount their existence, truth, or usefulness. The Devil discounted the Father's love for the Son in them. "If you are the Son of God," the Devil taunted. You are not a son like Jesus is. But make no mistake, you are a beloved child of God in Christ—real and true. You wrestle a fiend who wants to cause you doubt about who you are to the Father.

So you follow Jesus into the desert as a frame of reference for your quiet time. You write down or take note of all the reasons stored up in your thoughts that you are no longer loved by God, disowned as his child. You look to the Father through his Word to contemplate his love for you in Jesus. In this quiet time you wrestle lies about your being beloved. You place confidence in his promises.

You also talk openly to the Father about your desire to be everywhere for all. After all, to come to the Father by beholding his words, Jesus had to surrender the opinions of others, and so in your small way will you. Disappearing for forty days in the desert at that moment made little sense for Jesus. People would talk. With no phones or computers they were left to wonder, and he did not manage their discomfort. Jesus was not everywhere at once but with the Father in the desert with the Word.

That whole desert thing was slow too, "forty days, being tempted by the devil" (Luke 4:2). Every bone and muscle in our body addicted to immediacy will twitch and ache. No answers come quickly here. One day finished in the desert might be followed by another and then another and then another. In this kind of quiet time you take your cravings for immediacy to the Father for healing.

Jesus can fix his hunger if he just takes the bread (Luke 4:4). Jesus can prove that he is the Son of God if he just throws himself down (Luke 4:6). He can be the celebrity king possessing everything and inhabiting every place (Luke 4:5). Jesus sifts through all these ugly accusations, temptations, memories, fears, and lies to detect the Father's voice and stand there among the sentences. "It is written," he affirms. By this act, Jesus does what we cannot so that we too can sort through in the silence what the sentences affirm when everything devilish, beastly, and barren tries to tear us down or mislead us. This is a quiet time of a different kind. We behold God here among the thoughts we've not spoken and the emotions we've not vented in our attempt to be quick instead to listen. We learn once again in this quiet time of the desert that we are beloved. From there we return "in the power of the Spirit" to the place we've been given (Luke 4:14–15).

Beholding Changes the Way We Go to God's Word

I've written extensively about the ministry of the Word elsewhere.[12] Here I mention three implications for beholding God when we come to his Word.

First, the old Presbyterian pastor and professor Archibald Alexander described our study of the Bible as being one of hoping to receive the intended impression its words were meant to make upon our souls by God. "It is not the critic, the speculative or polemic theologian, who is most likely to receive the right impression," says Alexander, "but the humble, simple hearted, contemplative Christian."[13]

According to Alexander, whether we are "the most learned critic" or "the most profound theologian," we nonetheless come to the Bible as those who "learn to sit at the feet of Jesus in the spirit of a child."[14] We are Mary's pupil, learning from her to choose him as our portion, listening and learning at his feet, no matter how important our ecclesiastical world says we are (Luke 10:39–42).

When the threefold omni-temptation to be like God takes hold of us with speed, we gradually turn to the Bible as a tool kit to make our programs work or our sermons applaudable rather than as the words of our Beloved meant to help anyone anywhere find the way home.

But God forgive us. May he recover us again so that we relearn to open the Bible, not "as a common book, with a common and unreverant heart; but in the dread and love for God the author."[15] We open the book to behold not it but him as he is revealed to us in it. Soon the Bible becomes again for us like the drippings of the honeycomb, more appealing to us than any material gain or status in this world (Ps. 19:10).

Second, we need each other's help to remember that we are as the Ethiopian eunuch, needing to say, when our Bibles are open, How can I understand "unless someone guides me?" (Acts 8:31). We depend upon one another in community as this Ethiopian did with Philip. We cherish the books and commentaries, podcasts and conversations that help us understand God's words.

Yet let's not forget that while it would honor an author to have people open his book, quote him at length, and spend hours talking with others about what they thought the author meant, it would prove strange, even rude, if all this banter took place while the author was present in the room and no one ever said a word to him or looked in his direction. To behold God in his Word is to ask him directly what he meant by it. A desert parable comes to mind:

> The brethren came to Abba Anthony and laid before him a passage from Leviticus. The old man went out into the desert, secretly followed by Abba Ammonas, who knew that this was his custom. Abba Anthony went a long way off and stood there praying, crying in a loud voice, "God, send Moses, to make me understand this saying."[16]

Richard Baxter said it plainly: "Before and after you read the Scripture, pray earnestly that the Spirit which did indite it, may expound it to you."[17] An old pastor's wisdom also comes to mind: "If we aspire in earnest to a genuine contemplation of God, we must go I say, to the word."[18]

Beholding the Fruit of a Dream

But sometimes seasons of severe trial make this beholding God in his Word seem impossible. We can't find him. But he finds us. A rare scene from my own desert barren comes to mind. I had collapsed into a heap of ugly prayer amid a pile of messed tissues on the living room floor. I fell asleep and dreamt.

In the dream, I was supposed to preach but was so mind weary that I could not find the biblical text. But the people waiting for the sermon were hospitable to my disheveled condition. Each one called out to me Psalm 138 as my text. Someone came to the pulpit patiently and helped me find it. This scene seemed to repeat itself so that when I awoke I felt as if I had dreamt this all night. The words "Psalm 138" sunlit my heart.

I sat up on the living room floor and reached for my Bible. It was already open and piled from use with last night's tissues. The last several weeks I had cried as one alone in an empty room, my words falling dead to the ground with no one but the crows to pick at their carcasses. But now, each word left its warm impression—as if he was mine and I was his, and somehow his words on that page were indeed his present words of love to me. I wept as I read:

> I bow down . . .
>> and give thanks to your name. . . .
> On the day I called, you answered me;
>> my strength of soul you increased. . . .
> For though the LORD is high, he regards the lowly,
>> but the haughty he knows from afar.
> Though I walk in the midst of trouble,
>> you preserve my life;
> you stretch out your hand against the wrath of my enemies,
>> and your right hand delivers me.

> The LORD will fulfill his purpose for me;
>> your steadfast love, O LORD, endures forever.
>> Do not forsake the work of your hands. (Psalm 138)

All through that day I held this Scripture like a love letter. I cherished each word and felt the kisses of my true love tender upon the lips, cheeks, and forehead of my soul. I felt like a child gathered up into the strong arms of my glad-hearted Father who will provide for me and take up my cause even at his own risk. None of my circumstances had changed. Tear-worthy wreckage and slander still barked like the neighbors' dogs outside my windows and doors. But I was not alone. The Lord was near. And for the first time in a very, very long time, I knew this to be true. What I'd like you to see is not so much the dream itself but the fruit of it. A word to sustain me in my weariness was given.

Beholding God in Our Living Rooms

The first time I made contact with this beholding work of prayer, Word, and care in the ordinary, I didn't realize it. I was holding a teddy bear. "Let's say our prayers," Mamaw would say as she sat beside the bed. Then I'd close my eyes and fold my hands.

"Now I lay me down to sleep," I said. "I pray to the Lord my soul to keep. If I should die before I wake, I pray to you, Lord, my soul to take." I was a child at the time and prayed like one.

But thirty years later, hospice was in Mamaw and Papaw's house. It was spending the night with Mamaw in mind. "If I should die before I wake" was no longer the distant prayer of a boy and his teddy bear.

"Let's pray," I suggested. We sat in old chairs. Mamaw looked troubled.

"Is everything okay?" I asked.

She looked frightened and spoke as if she was about to confess a sin or a terrible event to me. "Today," she said. "I prayed for myself." Her lips trembled. Her eyes moistened.

"Do you think that was okay?" she asked. "Do you think it is okay with God that I prayed for myself today?"

As Mamaw's grandchild, I was struck tender deep. In all these years praying for others, Mamaw never risked a prayer for herself? I was dumbfounded with love for her.

But as a man, a pastor, I felt feisty and empowered to lean in, look clear into her eyes, and whisper grace words of spiritual direction to her tender conscience.

"Yes, Mamaw, it is okay in Jesus that you prayed for yourself. The Lord who loves you longs to hear your prayers, even those that have to do with you. You can cast all your personal cares upon him because he cares for you."

She nodded and we cried, smiling, beholding.

After Mamaw's funeral I was given her Bible as a gift. It rests here on my desk as I write.

She has bookmarks in several places. The hospice bookmark sits in John 17. The study Bible heading reads: "Jesus Prays for Himself." Mamaw has that heading circled.

Another bookmark sits at Isaiah 53, which foretells of Jesus the man of sorrows. Mamaw has highlighted in yellow the entire chapter.

The other bookmark takes us to Psalm 130. "Out of the depths I cry to you, O LORD! O Lord, hear my voice! Let your ears be attentive to the voice of my pleas for mercy" (vv. 1–2).

In my memory I see her there asking at death's door about what it means to please her Savior with prayer. I realize now that she was not just asking me but was earnestly asking God, going from promise to promise in his Word. Perhaps medicines, fatigue, cancer, and fear made his voice of love harder to hear, difficult to behold. So in this prayer and Word work together, I think of where we were—in a living room smelling of hospice, rocking in old chairs, from a story of long love, needing to locate God together.

I think to myself, *This is a gift, this small, mostly overlooked moment among the mattering things. A gift, I say, because God was there to be found, and he was.*

11

Finding Our Pace

You asked for burdens to carry—And howled when they were placed on your shoulders. Had you fancied another sort of burden?

DAG HAMMARSKJÖLD

Emotionally, we've sometimes worked a full day in one hour.

We've worn a whole week of worry into our prayers, and it's only Wednesday.

I was always told, "Watch out for emotions; you can't trust them."

But I've come to believe that my thoughts are no less shifty and just as impatient for attention.

Burdened For and Burdened From

An ambition for quiet leads us to learn how to behold God. Quiet beholding changes our pace. A pace conducive to the conditions we face can help us a great deal, because anxieties are coming.

Anxieties found me before I was a pastor. As my pop says, "I got them honestly." Bouts of anxiety apparently dapple the biology of my kin. Add to that my own share of providential trauma, and these anxious ants-in-the-pants moods that crawl about with their jitters and creepers are no surprise. What can surprise is that entering pastoral ministry does not un-anxiety us. The apostle Paul makes this plain: "Apart from other things, there is the daily pressure on me of my anxiety for all the churches. Who is weak, and I am not weak? Who is made to fall, and I am not indignant?" (2 Cor. 11:28–29).

Burdens can sit like sewage backed up into our basements or like a river overflowing banks into fields pushing toward our home. On such days the waters of stench or torrent will have to be dealt with. But pain or burden isn't always a crisis occasion. Sometimes a person's burdens are like arthritic fingers. We learn to open the pickle jar or turn the faucet each day with a wince. Our pastoral work takes us into the burdens that others bear as well as our own. These burdens generally come in two forms: burdens *for* and burdens *from*.

We are burdened *for*:

- Our families: "And seeing him, he fell at his feet and implored him earnestly, saying, 'My little daughter is at the point of death'" (Mark 5:22–23).

- Our neighbors and churches: "There is the daily pressure on me of my anxiety for all the churches" (2 Cor. 11:28).

- Our fellow ministers: "Lest I should have sorrow upon sorrow" (Phil. 2:27).

We are burdened *from*:

- Personal sin: "sinners, of whom I am the foremost" (1 Tim. 1:15).

- Limits and unanswered prayers: "Three times I pleaded with the Lord about this, that it should leave me" (2 Cor. 12:8).

- Our bodies: ". . . for the sake of your stomach and your frequent ailments" (1 Tim. 5:23).

- Our families: "And when his family heard it, they went out to seize him, for they were saying, 'He is out of his mind'" (Mark 3:21).

- Church members: "Alexander the coppersmith did me great harm" (2 Tim. 4:14).

- Fellow pastors: "Some indeed preach Christ from envy and rivalry" (Phil. 1:15); "There arose a sharp disagreement, so that they separated from each other" (Acts 15:39).

- Neighbors: "An attempt was made by both Gentiles and Jews, with their rulers, to mistreat them" (Acts 14:5).

One time after I led worship and preached, we walked out into the parking lot to discover that several of our cars had had their windows broken and personal items stolen. When I was in seminary I envisioned powerful sermons for which people would give thanks as the crowds gathered in appreciation, but I probably did not envision the pastoral care of a listening preacher, holding a broom to clear out busted glass in the rain and with humbled presence, holding a human being in tears. We found financial help to fix the burgled cars and mobilized visits for frightened thoughts. These burdens of life afford us pastors a profound privilege. We get to see God's merciful action firsthand and often. But we also can wear down without help, discouraged by the ironies of constant burdens and spiritual battles. (For example, the sermon that morning was from Ephesians 4:28, "Let the thief no longer steal.")

Moment by Moment
Jesus handles our anxieties with us by asking us to place them within a one-day-at-a-time pace for life.

> Therefore do not be anxious about tomorrow, for tomorrow will be anxious for itself. Sufficient for the day is its own trouble. (Matt. 6:34)

When my papaw labored through fluid-filled lungs in the last season of his life, I would call him on the phone.

"What do you know, young man?" he'd say. I could hear the wheeze of depleted breath in his voice.

"You are on my mind, Papaw. How is it going for you today?"

"Oh, I'm all right. It is what it is," he'd say. "Ain't no use in complaining, huh?"

Then he would add the piece of advice that had become familiar ground for him. He seemed determined to pass it on. "Just taking one day at a time," he'd say. "You know that's all we can do anyway; ain't that right, young man?"

I would pause in my own confounded attempts to practice in my being what he was saying. "Well, I think I have a lot to learn about that," I'd muster. I'd hear a smile in his voice, his lungs muscling through each bit of air.

"I love you, Papaw," I'd say.

"I love you too, Zack," he'd answer (words rarely uttered by him when he was a younger man but wonderfully and freely spoken now). Then he added what had become his regular request: "Don't forget to say a prayer for this old man."

"I won't, Papaw. I pray for you all the time," I'd assure him.

The Four Portions

Jesus gives us this gift of one-day-at-a-time portions to bear the burdens that find us. The psalmist gets us started in how to relearn that each day has enough of its own worry in it.

> Evening and morning and at noon
> I utter my complaint and moan,
> and [God] hears my voice. (Ps. 55:17)

Sometimes, the psalmist gets more specific about what "evening" can encompass, and, like other places in the Bible (e.g., Lam. 2:19), he refers to the night watches (Ps. 63:6).

The psalmist identifies four parts of a twenty-four-hour day. I've come to think of these four parts as portions. God is our portion, which means that at any given moment of our day he is there and is enough for us.

Morning: sunrise or 6:00 a.m. to noon

Noon: noon to 6:00 p.m.

Evening: sunset or 6:00 p.m. to 10:00 p.m. (sometimes known as the "first night watch")

The night watches: 10:00 p.m. to 6:00 a.m.[1]

Mark this down. In order to run a marathon we first have to run a mile. Running a mile is nothing to scoff at.

The Grace of the Morning

The New Testament tells us things about Jesus in the morning: he prayed (Mark 1:35). He was hungry. He walked (Matt. 21:18). He taught (John 8:2).

For the psalmist, the morning in God's hands testifies to us that tears end, relief is signified, and "joy comes" (Ps. 30:5). In the morning, songs of praise and thanksgiving can rise because God's strength has gotten us through the night (Ps. 59:16). The night didn't win. We awake and see once again that God's love hasn't quit on us, and we ask that he will go with us and guide us into what awaits us (Ps. 143:8). The morning stirs us to pray, therefore, and to watch how God will answer those prayers through the day (Ps. 5:3).

Morning is meant as a poem or sermon to console the downcast. It enables us to think again of God's goodness and to ask him why he waits to reveal that goodness to us (Ps. 88:13–14). The ending of night also rouses us to a renewed conviction to use the day as a means of opposing what is wretched in the world and protecting what is good and beautiful and right (Ps. 101:8). In fact, the sun is no morning melancholy like me, tired of shining again unnoticed, traveling the same old path every day and bored with it all. No! Because God gives this meaning to the morning, he poetically pictures the sun as a bridegroom lovestruck and happily longing to see his bride (Ps. 19:5). The sun shines love-stubborn above the thunderclouds.

Historically, it was the morning when Jesus's enemies bound his hands and determined to kill him (Mark 15:1). But poetically was there some hope the sunrise gave to our Lord as men possessed by the terrors of the night threw him out into the street? It was the morning. He knew it, didn't he? So many mornings he had known the intimacy of his Father. There had been many mornings before these ensnared men were born. Mornings would go on after they died. In fact, there would come a morning on the third day while it was still dark when death would die, these foul men would be confounded, and Jesus would rise again! The morning proclaims that resurrection and life have outlasted the night. Did that proclamation whisper to him? Was this part of the "joy . . . set before him" (Heb. 12:2)? Did the sun somehow wink at Jesus as they bound his hands and sought to take his breath away?

This is why I am coming personally to think of the morning as the time of grace. Of course, the whole day and night is dependent upon grace. I just mean that grace seems to rise to the forefront in the morning portion because we feel we are not enough to meet what awaits us; we wonder if the sun will shine in our circumstances the way it shines in the morning.

We rise; God's love is here! We pray; God's guidance is with us! We hope again and cry out anew; God is overcoming the darkness! We eat the daily bit we have; God has provided! We get to the work before us; God has something to show us! The dawn has come; the tomb is empty! The season of morning begins and ends. He has been our portion in our burdens until the noon comes. This is grace and accomplishment! We give praise to God. We've made it through the first mile of the day.

Noonday Wisdom

In the Psalms, "the noonday" symbolizes for God's people the light within which justice and virtue shine (Ps. 37:6). It is here that we act with wise choices regarding the work, the circumstances, and the persons at hand.

Therefore the afternoon fatigues us. It was at noon that Jesus, wearied from his journey, sat down for a break and a cup of water (John 4:6). The business of the day gets its second wind and picks up speed. Work must get done. Calls logged, tasks completed, e-mails written, meetings and agendas kept, fields plowed, bolts tightened, three more diapers to change, dinner to prepare, sickness to endure. Jesus poetically pictures the noon portion as "the burden of the day and the scorching heat" (Matt. 20:12). Work fusses us to its conclusion, paychecks are handed out, and the bones pop within our aching muscles.

Often, then, two hours after lunch the weariness sets in. For some of us, we experience the "noon-day demon," a dark cloud of mood that wriggles our legs, squirms us in our seats, and twiddles our thumbs. Such moods instill in us "a hatred for the place" we've been given, and "a hatred for manual labor."[2] It is little wonder that cocktails and happy hours tempt men and women of business in the afternoon. Distraction calls out to us.

No wonder the noon hour through 6:00 p.m. often puts virtuous paths to the test. If the morning is the time for taking our tears, plans, work, and questions of the day to his throne of grace and there finding hope, the afternoon seems to be the time of illumination in which our intention to lean on that grace is sifted and the true objects of our hope take off their masks.

At noon the sun is at its highest. It gives its strongest light by which to see, its strongest heat by which to be humbled. We are meant to resemble it. But Pilate faltered. And so did God's people.

It was in the noon portion that Pilate chose political advantage and ordered the innocent to be mistreated, the Son of God to die (John 19:14–15).

It was also at noon when Jesus breathed his last and the sun's light inexplicably failed (Luke 23:44). The dark and the sunlit noon traded places. They turned the day upside down as if to resemble the evil that was being called good, and the good that was being accused of evil.

If the morning beckons us to sing, the afternoon humbles us into a remembrance that we need his salvation. The morning teaches us to praise. The afternoon teaches us patience and perseverance. The noonday has a beginning and an end. To cross its finish line is grace and strength! Another mile and our burdens carried.

Evening Hospitality

Now when it was evening, the disciples came to him and said, "This is a desolate place, and the day is now over; send the crowds away to go into the villages and buy food for themselves." But Jesus said, "They need not go away; you give them something to eat." They said to him, "We have only five loaves here and two fish." (Matt. 14:15–17)

"The day is now over." The teacher and teaching come to a close. It is time for food and a bit of rest in the company of others who also are at rest and could likewise use a bite to eat. We needn't take our work with us. Workless in the evening matters.

Evening highlights hospitality. We extend the kindness and protection of a peaceable presence to our neighbors. It is kind because it takes our neighbors' bodily and soul needs into account and provides them room-giving acceptance and practical sustenance. Hospitality is also protective because remaining hospitable toward another means that we do not transgress, misuse, or consume them. We allow them to take up company in our presence in such a way that they know we will not use them to satisfy our lust or mandate that they act as if they are not tired or in need of nourishment.

The morning teaches us to sing. The afternoon teaches us to persevere. The evening teaches us to give thanks to God for the sacred boredom of mundane blessings that we can count (Ps. 141:2).

But the poetry of the Psalms also pictures the evening as shadow time (Ps. 59:6–7; 102:11; 104:23). After all, those whose afternoons were entertained by folly's seduction threaten hospitality. Happy-hour imaginations come to fruition in the evening (Prov. 7:7–9). Those who took no time to pause and take their foul moods to God prior to the evening's inauguration likewise rabble-rouse us. Irritable many of us come to our dinner tables. We litter the evening living room with the trash of our untended frustrations and anxieties. Those in our crowd pay for it without warrant—often and especially those closest to us, those whom we would say we love the most. In such cases, the dark of the evening emboldens the illicit misuse of one another. The dark gives rise to those who disregard God.

For this reason, our evenings need Jesus. Some evenings he went away to pray (Matt. 14:23). He acted as if he might go on. So we say to him with those on the road to Emmaus, "Stay with us, for it is toward evening and the day is now far spent." Like them, our hearts burn as he stays with us, breaks bread with us, and speaks of himself in the Scriptures for us (Luke 24:29–31).

In the evening, Jesus was hospitable to the sick and the demon possessed (Mark 1:32). Twice it was amid evening storms that Jesus showed his followers that he was with them amid what frightened them in the night (Mark 4:35; 6:37). Locked behind closed doors for fear of what the crucifying community would do to them, it was in the evening when Jesus pursued them and spoke to them, "Peace be with you," and made their hearts glad (John 20:19). Gladness for his goodness redeems the evening, and this is very kind of God, because the night watches are coming. How kind to direct our meditation to ordinary joys amid the glad company of neighbor love before the "night thieves" come to bogeyman us. Grace has come. Evening gave us gratitude. Burdens are carried. Another mile accomplished.

Solitude and the Night Watches

My soul will be satisfied as with fat and rich food,
and my mouth will praise you with joyful lips,

> when I remember you upon my bed,
>> and meditate on you in the watches of the night.
>> (Ps. 63:5–6)

I have always viewed solitude as a morning feature. But the poetry of the Psalms pictures the night watches as a place of solitude. Historically, when Jesus was up alone in the night in the desolate places of prayer, surely this testimony from Psalm 63:5–6 was the kind of portion that Jesus experienced with the Father (Luke 6:12).

The night watches picture for us a military soldier posted as lookout. The watchman stays awake and peers into the potential movements of the night to protect from enemies and guard the sleep of his people. He also watches for messengers or reinforcements who come bringing clarity or rescue by stealth. Bed for rest, watchfulness for clarity and rescue; sleep and sleeplessness—these are the movements of the deep night. Jesus accounts for these night watches in his parable:

> Therefore stay awake—for you do not know when the master of the house will come, in the evening, or at midnight, or when the rooster crows [3:00 a.m.], or in the morning. (Mark 13:35)

Solitude, silence, listening talk, and humble presence return to us. This is no "quiet time" in general, parsing out abstract truths. Solitude takes up with God the very real leftover emotions and questions from the day.

> Be angry, and do not sin;
>> ponder in your own hearts on your beds, and be silent.
>> (Ps. 4:4)

One purpose for our bed in the night is to ponder in our hearts what troubles us and to speak such things to God. Sleep results. Sleep is a Sabbath-like act. We rest from everything and leave it all for God's keeping while we lie motionless in the world for a while.

But there are terrors in the night too (Ps. 91:5). Nightmares. Sleepless weeping can linger (Ps. 30:5). Trouble can hold our "eyelids open" (Ps. 77:4). The desolate silence allows our heart questions to search in frenzied unrest (Ps. 77:7–9).

But it is also true that our unchecked afternoon folly can lead us into an inhospitable evening and fill our night watches with stumbling. "Come, let us take our fill of love till morning," the affair choosers say (Prov. 7:18). The predawn dark often haunts us with guilt and shame. We hail a cab half-drunk, with our dignity left for misuse in a stranger's bed, wondering what we were thinking. Or we pulled an all-nighter due to procrastination or over work. We have no sleep or solitude to strengthen us into the morning. The deep night then becomes a confessional, a school for God's counsel to find us and instruct us (Ps. 16:7).

> I rise before dawn and cry for help;
>   I hope in your words.
> My eyes are awake before the watches of the night,
>   that I may meditate on your promise. (Ps. 119:147–48)

Dreams in the Night

Some of us dream in the night, so let's pause here to remind ourselves about them. They come from one of three places, just as our thoughts do when we are awake. They can originate with us or with our enemy the Devil, or they are whispered to us by God. Either way, dreams are providential; that is, they too are one of the circumstances in our lives that God governs and through which he holds us for his glory and our true good (Job 33:15–18).

Whatever our dream, we take its contents and resulting thoughts and emotions to God. With him we can rest their poetic business and our frame of heart in Jesus. If there are persons in our dreams that stand out to us, we can intercede for them, just as we often do when persons come to our minds during our waking hours. We likewise entrust such fearful or celebratory impressions to him, believing that he will, as he always does, inform us, change us, and lead us according to his love and perfect timing in Jesus.

It was in the night watches that Jesus prayed with loud cries and tears in Gethsemane. He knows what it is to cry out in the dark. His empathy for us is deep when we too must learn this.

After the night and the dreaming, the dawn comes. The Lord who keeps you does not slumber but attends you (Ps. 121:4). The sun begins to break forth for his bride. A new day dawns. For a whole day now, he has carried you, burdens and all.

Our Daily Calendars

What practical difference does this four-portioned pace of a day make?

First, think of morning, noon, evening, and night as portions large enough for your attention and small enough to manage each day. No longer seek to blur them together or rush past them.

Second, as that portion of the day draws to a close, pause and look back before you start the new portion and rush forward. Give thanks to God for the tokens of his grace that you experienced. Or cry at the pains and lament. Or recognize your agitated moods and petition him about what originates them. Ask him to show you your errors, sins, and faults from that portion that he can lead you to confess and gratefully turn from. Or intercede for any situation or purpose that stuck out to you during that time. Then, out of this pause, praise him and ask him to lead you by the hand into the next portion of the day.

In this regard, let's say it's 11:47 a.m. The morning is about to rest. We look back and give thanks for what the morning brought to us. We pay attention to our moods too. Any foul mood, we trace back to what caused it. We locate that foul morning scene and cast it upon the Lord. Now, with his grace we await noon's arrival. We do not want to take unmeditated morning moods into the afternoon. Afternoon has enough of its own. Jesus carries our mornings.

Or the evening is coming. It's 5:30 p.m. or so (or 6:30 because we are behind). Food is simmering on the stove. Traffic awaits our commute home. We pause and reflect. We ask forgiveness; we seek his courage to make things right where we need to as much as it is possible with us; we give thanks for the strength he gave and for the morning prayers he answered; and we celebrate the virtue of his Spirit that, by his grace, lasted. We notice our aching muscles or tired brain. We seek his rest. We wrestle to believe our unfinished work will be there tomorrow waiting for us. The morning will give us time to take it to the Lord before it comes back around. It will all get done. For now, there are kids to play with, spouses to come alongside of, or family, friends, or neighbors to encourage. Leave the noon for now. Take its moods to Jesus so as not to unduly take them with you and hoist them upon others at the dinner table.

Or maybe, it's 9:45 p.m. Our table is cleared. The TV is turned off. Our kids are in bed (unless we have teenagers). Our friends are heading home. We pause to give thanks for the good food and company with which he has blessed us. We seek forgiveness for the foul moods we spilled upon others. We take heart that the morning will give us a new moment to take such things to him and hopefully sing and find praise again. We take our fears, our sickness, and our oppressions felt from the evening community to him. He stays with us and speaks peace. We brush our teeth. The time for bed approaches for some of us. For others, the time for quiet and prayer arrives. Third-shift jobs, hospital stays, seasonal parties, last-minute homework—each of these realities informs the night. But the second and third watches of the night are not normatively made for our TV watching, our leftover work from the day, or our after-party carousing, not as a norm anyway. The night is coming. The late night was made for our solitude with God. He waits with love to carry you.

When one portion ends and the other begins, it is as if we look back to gather up everything beautiful from the previous portion before moving on. These are like flowers scattered throughout that we gather up, put in our watered vases, and give thanks to God. We also gather up anything hard, painful, frightening, or sinful, like pieces of a shattered vase that we or someone else knocked off our tables. We broom these into a box and bring them before God.

Setting our flowers and broken pieces before God in this way, we give thanks and cast our cares. He holds these now, and we can move on into the next portion of the day.

Weekly Portions

One day in seven I seek to live these four portions as a day of rest. For twenty-four hours I am helped, apart from genuine emergencies, when I let e-mail and phone, appointments and pastoral work, all take a break. This has morphed over the years as my kids' ages have changed. But sometimes I sleep in. Or after kids are at school I watch an old movie or listen to music. Lunch is leisurely. Maybe I snooze in the afternoon before I pick up kids from school. I sleep with no guilt (at least, that is the goal). This is no waste of time. Not today.

But when weekly rhythms of rest are at their best for me, I find myself plopped on a blanket with a packed lunch. If it is late fall or early winter, I wear a cloth cap, gloves, and clothes warm enough to withstand three hours outside. In a plastic bag I have my Bible, some paper, and a stack of poetry or a novel. Nestled between the shade trees of one of my favorite sabbath-rest places, I look out over Creve Ceour Lake, or maybe I look down the long hill to the fountained waters of Forest Park. I wear tennis shoes and walk, maybe miles. Sometimes when it rains I just sit in my old red truck looking out over the lake.

Here in this mundane place among these mattering things, I'm surrendering into listening again. I'm listening for God. Laying my burdens down. Being taken up by him. Grateful and glad laughs return. Sometimes I cry awhile without fully knowing why. But he does. These burdens are his.

When I've lost track of sabbath Fridays or Mondays and I am irritable and worn out for their lack in my life, I've noticed that one day of rest won't provide much rest at all. A sort of detox need returns. I have to remember that humbled presence, listening talk, and solitude among these weekly portions have a cumulative effect; just as it is with the four portions of a day. Once I begin to get several daily and weekly portions in a row into my pace again, the change in my being grows noticeable. My burdens may have increased. But I'm able again to offer rest and hospitable presence for others because I actually possess something of this myself. The grace of this amazes me.

When I first introduced the idea of "resting months" to our congregation, they didn't like it. Three months a year we'd give all our weekly ministries a break without guilt (April, August, and December). I did this because of the age of our congregation, made up of mostly young families with kids. These same families were doing all the volunteering at the church and in the community. Between serving and volunteering, going to Bible studies and house groups, people were wearing out. On the flip side, if anyone did take a break they felt enormous guilt, like they were letting God and us down. Of course, we don't mandate that our members observe resting months; people can keep meeting if they desire to. But over the years, most have grown thankful for the built-in rhythm they provide. We strategically rest in order to vigorously keep going. If we don't, we wind up taking unplanned breaks because we are sick or burned out from overworked schedules.

Pacing Ourselves

How then do these daily and weekly portions help us? A small scene of a story gives us an answer. Nate and his dad poised themselves to trek a difficult mountain. Nate tells us the story.

"Nate, I think if we move at a really slow pace we won't have to stop as often. Here, watch."

My father moved his feet methodically, slow but steady.

"Dad, you're crazy!" I laughed. We'll never get there. Look how slow you're walking. I could crawl faster. You look ridiculous!"

"Do what you want," he muttered. "I'm going to walk slowly!"

I brushed off my father's wisdom and raced ahead up the mountain. After about a half hour of hiking up a steep pitch, I noticed that, with all my painful stops, he was keeping up with me. I felt exhausted. Dad didn't stop even once, and he seemed to be gliding up the mountain.

As is often the case in life, pain made me teachable. That day it was burning lungs and shaky legs. . . . I gave Dad's theory a try and joined his ridiculously slow march. I soon discovered that if I kept going slowly, it was easier not to stop. I couldn't believe it. There on the side of the mountain one of my lifelong quandaries was being revealed. The answer was just so simple.

Pace yourself.

Move slowly.

Don't stop.[3]

PART FOUR

Reshaping the Work We Do

12

Care for the Sick

The visitation of the sick . . . is of the highest importance. . . . Lessons are learned here that could never be
learned in the study.

Charles Bridges

In the second year of my first pastorate, I began singing songs and
leading a weekly Bible study at a local assisted-living facility for the
elderly. After the study and the song, the eyes of one elderly woman
glistened with tears. She walked toward me, kissed my cheek (the
way many of these older ones did), and thanked me. I kissed her
cheek in return. This was their custom, not mine, and admittedly I
felt uncomfortable. But I gave her a hug and took a moment to pray
for her. She gave thanks to God. I thought nothing more about it.

The following Wednesday after the study and the song, I rose
from the piano and was dumbfounded to notice that a line of men
and women immediately formed. Each one seemed to wait for their
turn. The aged women kissed my cheek, the silver-headed and bald-
ing men shook my hand. I awkwardly returned these gestures and
prayed for them. Hugs blossomed. Smiles unfolded like petals; tears
moistened and accumulated as if soaked by the dew of a sunlit
morning. Strange!

Over the months, this kind of line forming for touch and prayer faded into a kind of normative community practice. Those Wednesday mornings, the many funerals that followed, this tender way of neighbor care and gratitude to God in Jesus—these became to me like the treasured drawings and pictures that persons sometimes magnet to their refrigerator.

The People Who Teach Us

Touch forms part of our pastoral work. I've mostly been awkward and alert in this work, on the lookout for inappropriate touch. I will talk about this hazardous kind of touch in the next chapter. But the Lord began to teach me about the good kind of touch each week.

I remember Betty, in a hospital bed, her mouth covered with a mask that spoon-fed her lungs with breath. The steady beeping of an apparatus indicated the dripping of medicine into the taped tubes of her veins. I fumbled for a Bible passage to read, nervous with youth, unsure of how to glimpse Jesus for the eighty-year-old widow as she lay pressed beneath it all. Before I said a word, Betty raised her tube-laced arms and managed a sentence beneath her mask. "Shall we pray, Pastor?" She said this less like a question and more like a statement. Looking back, I now believe that this old saint was teaching me what my role for such a moment was meant by God to be. She was mentoring me. I took her hand and held it. I laid my other hand lightly upon her forehead. There together, in Jesus's name and with his present empowerment, I strongly raised my feeble voice to God.

Before Betty raised her hand for prayer in her hospital room that day, she had already taught me something good about the occasional human touch between men and women who in Jesus are united like family. Admittedly, I saw her as more grandmotherly than sisterly. But even here I had learning to do, and I think she saw that. To her I was her pastor—grandson-like, yes, but still a man of God sent to do her good in Jesus. Though I often secretly feared that I would be found out as somewhat boyish in the wise presence of the elderly, she saw me as the grown man I was. She treated me according to the calling I had been given. This always humbled me.

Anyway, it was the anniversary of her husband's death. He had died more than twenty years before. She asked if we could sit and talk for a moment. All of a sudden the dam broke and the tears poured through. We sat. She wept. My shoulder held her fatigued head and bolstered her heaving torso. I did not know what else to do. I prayed while she cried.

It turns out there was nothing else to do. I had not imagined before this how little a widow experiences touch as it is meant to be. Family members live at a distance and visit sporadically. Beyond the pokes of medical people, the elderly often enter a famine of touch as if dwelling in the desert years of their lives. Upon whose shoulder does a widow lean when she grieves the loss of the husband she loved? Only once was I that shoulder for Betty. And that is probably how it should be. But it reminded me of the role that we play for one another in community. My shoulder was safe and strong. For a moment it brotherly pillowed her genuine grief. I hope one day a gospel shoulder might kindly let me lean upon it amid my own fainting for the loved one I lost, as I too wait for heaven's glad reunion in Jesus to find me.

Not surprisingly, Betty was one of those in line by the piano early on. I look back now and recognize that I was too awkward with this touch of the right kind. Men and women formed a line because safe and brotherly human touch was like a rare gem. A handshake, a hug, presence, a kiss on a cheek, prayer—human touch the way a family is meant in Christ to offer one another—was a treasured commodity to take advantage of while it lasted.

In my case with Betty, Paul gives the category for us. Young men are to treat older women as mothers, which implies that older women treat younger men as sons (1 Tim. 5:2). The "mother" found a moment for the shoulder of a "son."

Gospel touch, then, is meant to resemble the touch normatively appropriate between family members. This is your guide. Pastoral care for the soul has to account for the body too. Therefore, abusive, neglectful, presumptuous, or sensual touch has no place in the touch of gospel life and ministry. (Those of us who have only such categories of damaging touch need the healing grace and mentoring of Jesus before we attempt familial touch in Jesus's name. Until the gospel rightly changes our use of touch, we are less ready for ministry than we realize, no matter how gifted we are to teach or preach or counsel.)

Jesus and the Touching of the Sick

The contact of Jesus's skin with the stuff of earth dots the pages of the Gospels: bread and fish, a basin of water, a towel, a cup, wine, wheat, tree bark and tables, lilies in a field. Jesus is the one who gathered dirt into his hands, spit into it with his saliva, hand-rubbed the brew into mud, and slathered the damp grit onto the broken eyes of a man born blind (John 9:6).

Jesus touched the sick and often on the wound. Jesus touched the leprosy of the leper (Matt. 8:3), the ear of the deaf (Luke 22:51), the eye of the blind, the hand of the feverish (Matt. 8:15), and the tongue of the mute (Mark 7:33). This was *pitiful* touch (Matt. 20:34), the caress of pity.

No wonder "all who had diseases pressed . . . to touch" Jesus (Mark 3:10). Such touch, like a righteous army, thoroughly routs the abuse and neglect of enemy hands that intend harm to the infirmed. We the sick long for this Jesus touch that defends and comforts. Such touch either heals us now or meaningfully signifies the healing that with heaven will come. Though it may delay, in Christ healing will not ultimately falter. The touch of Jesus's pity preaches such hope.

For this reason, Jesus will lead us in our lives and ministries into the sickbed smells of medicated bones among muscles drunk with prescribed concoctions. The widow rooms and cancer wards of each community reveal for us where Jesus will surely visit. We the frightened or hardened need Jesus to take us by the hand and guide us toward the sick within our families or congregations or communities. Any adult whose life stage has transitioned her into the role of primary caregiver for her parent knows that we cannot care for the sick alone. Any family member who lives hours away or any pastor who can be only at one place at one time among an aging congregation needs help to remember that we are not Jesus, and our ability for care is more limited than we would like. There are too many people and too much ailment for our two shoulders. But in Jesus a community of shoulders can substantially touch the sick, literally and figuratively.

Ours may be not to touch the wound directly as Jesus does. And never do we touch anyone who does not wish it done. But when we pray for the sick, we can ask, "May I take your hand and pray?" Or for the critically infirmed we can gently lay our hand softly upon the head or arm. A gentle pat on the shoulder with a kind word or a hug can go a long way for those who can still stand.

Gravesides

Pastoral care is mostly presence, being with someone in the midst of what troubles them. Touch of the right kind is a sentence. Or sitting on a chair in the room while family members gather is our paragraph. In pastoral care, eye contact, a small nod or shaking of the head, a tear, a smile, a willingness to hold an umbrella over a grieving one's head in the rain, a willingness to cut bread for sandwiches, a commitment to help the foggy head of weeping make decisions without deciding for them—all this describes an awkward and imperfect stamina for growing present among people without trying to draw attention or make something happen or artificially conjure up a God moment; these more than your words form the tools of your vocation of care.

My very first funeral as a pastor was for a neighbor whom I did not know. I hear the director come to me in the separate room. "It's time," he says. I hear my stomach growl. I hear the sound of my shoes on well-worn carpet. I hear myself try to patch words of life together for those who are mostly strangers to me. I hear myself begin to tremble a voice out into the devastated crowd.

At the time, I actually had little acquaintance with the sounds of death. The years since have changed all that, but it was the first such occasion that I heard the bagpipes sound. After the service, out by the graveside, the bagpiper stood as if ugly and holding a goose. He breathed in and out into a moaning that wheezed air into a haunting melody of "Amazing Grace." The wind rippled through the fall leaves. Rented aluminum poles clanked with rope and tarp. I heard the sound of flowers dropped on a casket. A military funeral, the flag folded and given, rifles armed for different use; death bullets shocked the silence to honor a life. I remember then how strange it was to encounter grown men and women heaving with pained gasps. Waves of sniffles like the tide sounded back and forth in gentle laps. Clichés hurried to put costumes onto the awkward silences. Questions about God or life whispered in embarrassment or raged into sudden bursts. Laughter emerged often in the strangest places for a comfort that's not strange at all.

Pat had died. Her sister brings a story to my ears.

"Pat used to find stray cats and give them a home," she says.

I chuckle with this surprising introduction and begin to smile.

She continues. "Pat would not only give these cats a home; she'd also dress those darn cats with clothes—doll clothes!"

"Really?" I ask.

"Oh, yes!" she says. She begins to laugh as she thinks about what her heart knows of happier times. I begin to laugh too.

"So, here's Pat, with all these dressed-up cats, posing for a picture, and Pat smiling from ear to ear!"

We're both laughing hard now and depending on tissues to maintain decorum.

"Oh my, that Pat! She sure was a loon!"

We laugh hard for a moment and then take a deep breath into a sudden downshift. The storyteller now stares off and quiets into silence. Without looking me in the eyes, she says, "I'm gonna miss that Pat."

Listening to these stories of memory is your work. When someone tells you about a deceased loved one, ask gently what the loved one's name was. Linger here and listen. When you greet someone who is grieving, there is no need to say, "How are you doing?" or "How is your day?" This question forces a person into the puzzle of putting unexplainable realities into a sentence. If we stop and think about it, we likely already know how these hurting ones are doing. Instead, we greet by simply saying something like, "I'm grateful to see you; you've been on my mind," or, "I've been praying for you; you are loved by us all." And as a norm we don't ask, "What can I do for you?" because the question puts the sick one in charge of managing your schedule and coming up with tasks. So we learn to offer something specific that lends itself to a yes or no answer, like, "May I bring you coffee in the morning?" or, "Would you like to rest today?" or, "Would it help if I picked up your daughter from school tomorrow?" Such specifics also help us resist our temptation to ask what we can do, not for their sake, but for ours, because we feel so helpless and we want to make it different than it is. I know this temptation too well. But if they could, they would make it different too. So there we are, each of us looking to Jesus in the frazzled quiet together.

In your sermon, therefore, you speak from the quiet of having listened and loved. You say something like this:

I understand that Pat was always on the lookout for stray cats.

At this, those who love her giggle with memory.

In fact, did I hear it right that Pat would not only give these cats a home but also dress them up in dolls' clothes?

Now the laughter of love pours through the tears of loss among those who knew her. I too am laughing now with gratitude. The laughter lingers for a while. Then the tears recover their place, and the quiet returns.

You know, when I think of how Pat wanted to give strays a home and clothes and how proud she was to call them her own, I can't help but think about a story that Jesus told about sheep scattered and lost. He said that God was like a shepherd searching to find them and bring them home. Thank you for telling me this story about Pat and your love for her. She reminds me of my own need to be found again and given a home. All of us need finding. Before she got sick, Pat shared how she had been lost all those years but that Jesus had finally found her. He can find us too and bring us home.

Calling for the Elders to Pray

Is anyone among you sick? Let him call for the elders of the church, and let them pray over him, anointing him with oil in the name of the Lord. (James 5:14)

At the churches I've served over the years, we've sometimes set aside a day for prayer. Alongside these regular public gatherings, sometimes the call comes, and we gather in a living room or by a hospital bed.

"Let him call," James says. His words bring to mind the bent-boned and the eye-blind, those who sit on mats forgotten by the sides of roads. News would reach these wheezy-lunged and sore-skinned human beings. "Jesus is coming!" they heard. "Jesus is drawing near!"

Abrupt to find their voice, these blood-coughed persons tried to garble a word out or knee-crawl on pebbled dirt to touch a thread of Jesus's garb. Either way, arthritic or tremulous hands finger-fought to raise the banner of their heart cry, "Son of David, have mercy on me!" He responds, and we learn that in Jesus the sick have a voice. Their call resembles nothing of nuisance or bother. In Jesus's mind, the mentally harassed and body weary are not shoved to the outskirts. There is little surprise, therefore, that praying for the sick is asserted by James in an elder's job description. Elders are not Jesus. But these returning ones are shepherds given to glimpse and resemble for others the presence, teachings, tone, and expression of the true and good Shepherd who knows his sheep by name (John 10:3). They hear his voice somehow in ours.

Sometimes there are two of us. Other times there are more, along with friends or house-group members who tiptoe into the room, nervous with love for the one who suffers. One of the elders, a maintenance man by day, reaches his dirt-creased knuckles into his pocket for the oil. He hands it to the pastor. The oil was bought at a local bookstore. It smells like incense. But any oil will do, for the oil is like the dirt in the maintenance man's hands. The dirt is not the work but a signal of the work that was done. Both the dirt and the oil offer no defense for soap. Both will release their grasp from the skin and wash away into the sink or tub drain that night. But though the symbol disappears, the work it revealed remains. Like Old Testament anointing, a setting apart has taken place.

The work to be done has to do with "the name of the Lord." There is no incantation or spell here. One can recite the words "in Jesus's name" and still know quite little of what it means to pray in the name of the Lord. Name dropping is a tool used by the arrogant to show others their resources, friendships, and connections. Among the humble, name dropping is rarely used except when a need arises that no other remedy can meet. The prayer in his name is a declaration that only Jesus possesses the wisdom, the resources, the provision, and the power to govern what ails us. (Even our good use of medicine and our active gratitude for good doctors and nurses are like shoes ultimately held together by the stitching and laces of God.)

The Prayer of Faith

At some point, one of the elders explains these things briefly to the one who has called. Then the one who has called expresses, if he or she can, what is being asked of Jesus. Then, amid flip-flops or loafers, coffee breath and sniffles, an elder dabs oil on his finger or thumb, touches the forehead of the sick, in silence or with words

(James gives no directive). If with words, it can sound in substance something like this:

> Barbara, Jesus belongs to you. You belong to him. He alone can save you and mend you. Through him you were created. By him you have been rescued. For him you now live by his grace. You are a daughter of the King. We take up your cause with him. His throne is one of grace. Let us go to him in this time of need.

Then the prayers of faith begin. Different elders pray, quietly and out loud, in turn or all at once (according to cultural custom), as others in attendance pray alongside. A prayer of faith has no requisite tone of voice or body posture. God hears us not because we are loud or soft. There is no amount or type of words. God hears us not because we use enough words or the grandest words. Faith is "the assurance of things hoped for, the conviction of things not seen" (Heb. 11:1). In Jesus, elders pray with assurance and conviction, even if as only possessing a mustard seed of both.

But why must faith attend the elders' prayers? This is no last-rites kind of praying. The elder talks to the Lord as one who sees a future in Jesus for the sick person. There is another side to this sickness. It will not have the last word!

> The prayer of faith will save the one who is sick, and the Lord will raise him up. (James 5:15)

To believe that the Lord rules over the mud that mucks us up and can say a word to heal us challenges elders. Sometimes we see with our human eyes in that moment only men, women, and children who are sick-bent, thought-haunted, or brain-broken. And when our only tangible piece of sacredness is a bit of oil that we bought for $5.95 down the street, it can seem that our words fall pummeled from the sky in a blitzkrieg of disease. After all, we who are praying just finished a burger and fries in the car on our way over here.

But "Elijah was a man with a nature like ours," James reminds us. "The prayer of a righteous person has great power as it is working," he assures us (James 5:16–17). Our faith is not in our words, our emotions, our worked-up agitation, or our limited and frail nature. Our faith is in the Lord, whose will and wisdom and power are able to sustain our loved ones in their suffering or to free them partially or altogether from it.

I have prayed in this fashion for many people over the years (though not as many as I could have, due to my early fears about the spookiness of faith-healer misuse of such people and such texts). And yet on most of those occasions, when I've prayed as an elder in this way, the prayed-for healing has not come. It seems to me that we pray with faith either way—faith that God can mend us with a word in an instant, and faith that God can sustain us by his grace even if he does not remove our suffering (Luke 22:42) or leaves us with our ailment (2 Cor. 12:8–9).

Confessing and Forgiving

No wonder James shifts gears from the healing of the body to the healing of the soul.

> And if he has committed sins, he will be forgiven. Therefore, confess your sins to one another and pray for one another, that you may be healed. (James 5:15–16)

While sickness can indicate on rare occasions the presence of sin as a cause (1 Cor. 11:30), on most occasions sickness has nothing to do with individual sin (Job 2:1–7; John 9:1–3) but rather represents the fact that Eden is broken and heaven is not yet.

But when sickness yells at us and taunts like a bully, and no one comes to rescue us, there in the mud we begin to see things in the thoughts and emotions of our inner being that we did not realize—ugly things that reveal that we are not as righteous as we once thought. We see our need for a savior all the more. We begin to confess. The sickness of body or mind throws a brick at the mirror of our perfect image. We see our reflection shattered and find ourselves more needy for grace and the merit of Jesus than we ever knew when our joints and muscles worked.

It won't be long. Not really. Likely, I, too, in time will lie beside the road, scooted to the outskirts of community, crying out, "Son of David, have mercy on me!" With hope I imagine some young pastor feeling awkward and some ordinary elders with their coffee breath and their Bibles coming to my bedside in the name of Jesus. I will hear them beseech my Lord on my behalf. Their presence, their empathy, their good touch, and their tenacity to lay hold of that which I cannot see, their gracious reception of my newfound confessions of my true need for forgiveness, will lead me to Jesus. The throne of grace awaits. These sickened bones on this couch or bed on which I will lie cannot and will not keep me from it.

13

Care for the Sinner

These eyes—holes of a mask.

JOHN UPDIKE

Sunday mornings there was a man who regularly gave "holy kisses" to various women in the congregation when he greeted them at the doors of morning worship. Over time, whispers of complaint began to find my ear. Two women in particular finally and awkwardly described that the kiss felt no resemblance to what is holy.

In the New Testament, two kinds of physical touch are set in brutal contrast. The first is Judas's kiss of Jesus's cheek. This kind of kiss misuses physical touch in order to consume or preserve its own selfish wants, lusts, desires, or agendas (Luke 22:47–48). It misuses adults and children under the guise of a "holy kiss" in God's name. In contrast, the "holy kiss" of the New Testament envisions a way for Christian community to recover in Jesus how human beings were originally meant to touch each other.[1] Few of us know in an experiential way what it means to touch or be touched in a sacred way. Profane touch has mentored and broken most of us.

These two kinds of touch form a picture of a pastor's two kinds of care, not only for the sick but for sinners. When I spoke of my desire for ministry, and Jesus asked me what I wanted him to do for me, I never would have said, "Please teach me what it means to care for the sick and for the sinner with my life. Please enable me to do this in such a way that your love for both is resembled in my ways."

Discipline and Sin

In my oral exams for ministry, I stood before fifty elders and was asked, "What is the purpose of church discipline?"

Fresh out of seminary, and in line with my theological tradition, I answered that "the purpose of church discipline is to uphold the character and teaching of Jesus and to protect the welfare of his flock."

Afterward a gentle and seasoned pastor caught up to me in the hallway and asked if he might suggest a fuller answer. "There is a third purpose for church discipline," he said kindly. "That third purpose has to do with the welfare of the one who sins. This is good news for any of us."

"Right!" I said. "I forgot about that one."

Over the years, I've come to understand that when someone is caught in a sin, we can still forget this one.

Relating to the Hardened

Sometimes our combustible response rises because the sinner defends his sin. For nearly two years I tried to meet with the man who gave profane "holy kisses." We had asked him to stop. Not long after, an affair came to light, and his marriage lay tattered in the darkness. I was awkward and imperfect, but I appealed to him with two messages. First was the message that we would do everything we could to walk with him and his family through this terrible brokenness for the testimony in years to come that God could give them in Jesus. The second message was that in time his continuous refusal to admit his actions as contrary to the gospel would put his correspondence to Jesus in question and require us to painfully say so. He eventually wrote this to us:

Unless you consider man's laws to be of higher authority than God's laws, the adultery began in November 1979 and will end in 2000. My wife is not my wife, Luke 16:18. Referencing your meeting, I no longer consider you my church. . . . Youth carry no importance in your church, no one in the last seven months has extended a hand to my children during this time. Jesus's response to what is the greatest commandment was, "You shall love your neighbor as yourself," Matthew 22:39.

When someone refuses to admit wrongdoing (including us), we use all our reasoning to justify it. In this note, this sane and biblically respected and dear man actually called his marriage of twenty-one years adultery. He reasoned that because his marriage had been performed by a justice of the peace rather than by a pastor, his marriage wasn't recognized by God. In his mind, the Bible supported and commended his having an affair and leaving his wife. Someone using the Bible in this way can ignite our impatience.

We can also struggle because when someone refuses to admit wrong, they take the moral high ground and believe themselves more righteous than others. In this case, he attacked us for leading poorly while, as a church leader, he himself was having an affair and biblically defending it. He attacked us for not caring for his kids while, as a dad, he was cheating on their mom and separating from them. He saw potential specks in our eyes while the log in his remained undetected.

In all this we can also struggle simply because blame-shifting hurts. We wished our youth group was better too. We were reaching out to his wife and his kids but felt terribly inadequate. We prayed and tried—made meals, went to coffee, sent notes. It is hard to take such arrows from one who is shooting everyone around him and needing help himself.

Start with Ourselves

Entering another's brokenness can expose us. Maybe we are afraid of our spouse leaving us. Maybe we were the child of a dad who left our mom for another woman. Maybe we have been secretly thinking about the breakdown of our own marriage and eyeing the woman who sits two pews over every Sunday. Our emotional reaction can pull us by the hair. Seeing him causes us to look at things in ourselves that we'd rather not.

Some of us grow passive. We light the long fuse and then run for cover behind distant shelters. Our blasting of sinners is done through our neglect rather than our actions—what we omit rather than what we commit. Our business, we say, was elsewhere. We arrange life as a ministry leader so that we can live the lie of never having to say we are sorry to anyone.

No wonder Paul says, "Keep watch on yourself, lest you too be tempted" (Gal. 6:1). Have you ever heard yourself say, "I would never do that"? There is a trapdoor in that sentence.

When my pastor friend took his own life, several people in the ensuing months confessed to me that suicide was on their mind. Someone did it. The broken church had to walk fatigued and numbed through it all again.

When my first marriage was imploding, and I was scrambling desperately for help, there was one man who repeatedly counseled me that a divorce wasn't so bad. I later learned that his own marriage was deeply troubled. His counsel, rather than being biblical, was tainted with his own temptations.

I remember a man sharing with me the porn sites he used. He did so as an act of confession to "bring it into the light." But the web-address names taunted me to click on them for the next three days.

> If anyone thinks he is something, when he is nothing, he deceives himself. But let each one test his own work, and then his reason to boast will be in himself alone and not in his neighbor. (Gal. 6:3–4)

The Unavoidable Predicament

The former leader ended his marriage and kept on with his new mistress. It was not a private kind of sin that could be dealt with in a merely private way. His was public, and everyone was watching. He was our friend. We were deeply pained. Some wanted swift action and vehemence. We resisted that notion. We would err on the side of giving too much time for him to come to his senses, if we were to err at all. Nearly two years of appealing, walking with, and attempting to help had passed to no avail. We had no success in gaining our dear brother (Matt. 18:15). He refused to listen (v. 17). We had to "let him be" to us as a "Gentile and a tax collector" (v. 17).

What did this mean? I didn't know. So, I looked in the Gospels for how Jesus related to Gentiles and tax collectors. From his way, it was clear that we would love this man. We would say hello and talk about the weather if we saw him at the store. Perhaps he would say, "Can we get together for coffee?" We would say, "Sure, but on my mind is the welfare of your heart. When we meet, can we also talk about that?" "No," he might respond. "Okay," we would say. "I pray for you and long for your good. Anytime you would like to talk about things, I'd welcome coffee with you. But, honestly, I need Jesus too. And I'm still hoping you will be able to admit what you've done with your family isn't what Jesus would have for us and that you will want to fall into the arms of Jesus's grace."

When Paul says of the hardened sinner who calls himself a Jesus follower, "Don't even eat with such a one," he does not invite us to meanly shun or disregard or mistreat such a one. Rather, a meal would sit like a gift on our table if the person would see his need for forgiveness. We long for this. But we wait for it. Our love, longing, kindness, and prayers for him cannot take away the reality that in Jesus the man is now identified "as if" he is no longer part of the believing community. Our fellowship is neither what it was nor what it could be.

We recognize his marriage is likely (though not certainly) lost for good. But what joy and freedom it would mean to simply say, "I know I was wrong. I need forgiveness and change." The community could then join in with him with tears but also glad hope!

He could also still bless his kids with wise instruction. He could remove the crazy-making from them—the idea that Jesus says it's right for daddies to leave their mommies for another woman, the notion that such a teaching puts in their heads about who they are as daughters who will one day become women. Clarity could take his kids' hands to walk down surer paths for their futures.

And he could still say to his former wife, "I was wrong. Please forgive me." They may never return even to a posture of friendship. But simple admission can take the lightning and the thunder out of the storm clouds that will drape the skies of their mutual parenting.

Most importantly, the honor of Jesus and his teachings would find clarity again in his public life for all who watched him. In his heart, before God, he would be reconciled. All that energy to twist Bible verses, to invert the moral high ground, and to blame-shift can cool down. The muscles of each minute can relax. The heartbeat of each second can slow down. To be "gained" again in Jesus. To defend neighbor love and to find rest for the soul—these blessings would reveal the third purpose of discipline's bearing its sweet fruit in an ordinary life.

Relating to the Softened

Surprisingly, we can struggle to relate not just with the resistant but also to the one who admits wrongdoing and actively seeks forgiveness. To begin, we want the person who sinned against us or against our community to hurt. If he confesses his wrong too quickly, we feel it is unfair. Our emotions are just getting started. What do we do with them if we can't throw them at the offender?

Also, when someone is actually changed by grace, it requires us to change, not just them, and we do not like this. Imagine a husband and wife. The husband has struggled with anger for years. She has prayed for him. After all this time Jesus begins to change him. During their next argument, she treats him as if he is expressing anger unlovingly the way he always has. The problem is, he is actually loving her quite well. Suddenly, she is the one who is out of bounds in the way she is treating him in the moment. Now, he is the hurt one. She is the one who needs to ask forgiveness. Answered prayer for him now invites her to change too.

But she doesn't like this. He has poorly expressed his anger for years. She should be allowed to for once! Instantly she is tempted to remove the welcome mat from the answered prayer. It makes sense why. After all, she can no longer talk about her husband in the way she always has. Her prayer requests for her husband at women's group have to change. She no longer has a reason to avoid attention to her own issues. All this time he was the defensive and impatient one. Now she finds that she is defensive and impatient—not because he is mean but because he is gracious!

Sometimes going to a new place of gospel freedom together is lovely to dream about and frightening to take hold of.

Listen to how Paul writes to confessing ones:

> I wrote to you out of much affliction and anguish of heart and with many tears, not to cause you pain but to let you know the abundant love that I have for you. (2 Cor. 2:4)

His posture is tearful, full of longing and concern for their well-being. They are dear to him. His purpose is expressly designed not to hurt them but to strengthen their sense of how loved they are in what they still have to learn and confront.

In fact, Paul initially regretted that he wrote to them, feeling he had hurt them wrongly (2 Cor. 7:8). He clarifies his thankfulness that they were not pained by him in the wrong way. "As it is, I rejoice, not because you were grieved . . ." (2 Cor. 7:9).

Paul's posture is nothing like the wrongful dad who spanks and spanks and spanks a child until he is certain the child has hurt enough for the sin committed, as if making someone feel conviction of sin is his and not the Holy Spirit's job (John 16:8–9). He does not want the child to ever forget what he has done (which translates into always needing to wear the grey overcoat of having sinned and never being able to dress in the bright clothes of forgiveness).

In contrast, Paul points out that because the one who was caught in sin is actually being changed, the community too must act accordingly.

> For such a one, this punishment by the majority is enough, so you should rather turn to forgive and comfort him, or he may be overwhelmed by excessive sorrow. So I beg you to reaffirm your love for him. (2 Cor. 2:6–8)

Punishment for the repentant does not go on and on. We resist the excessive sorrow of the repentant heart with the gospel. "Forgive, comfort, reaffirm your love," Paul pleads.

Forgiveness will not justify folly or remove all consequences. There is no way that a person who hates the molestation he committed, even though forgiven, will ever have charge of the nursery. His place in the community will require he use his gifts in other ways.

Friendship does not always follow from forgiveness among those victimized. Though able to forgive by grace, the harmed one may attend a different church from the one who hurt her or vice versa. Rarely does forgiveness have a fairy-tale ending in the moment, but it does lead us toward a redemptive ending for everyone involved—an ending that heaven will fully mend into completion.

But why does all this matter anyway? Because, according to Paul, how we handle the repenting sinner now is an act of spiritual warfare. These situations "test" us regarding the extent of our obedience (2 Cor. 2:9). Obeying by forgiving and reaffirming our love for the repentant one is necessary to fight against the "designs" of Satan in the community (2 Cor. 2:11). It is Satan and not God who inflicts excessive sorrow upon a repentant person, along with the absence of love, the neglect of comfort, and a punishment that never ends. At this point Paul reminds us, therefore, that when dealing with discipline and sin, we are tempted to reflect more of a devilish than a divine approach.

Discerning the Sorrows

Light a match for a fire pit while camping, and both gasoline and newspaper will ignite. Both are capable fire starters for dinner. Both are capable destroyers of the campsite. But one of them is volatile and not to be trusted.

Likewise, both the Devil and God talk about sin. But their impact differs dramatically. While the Holy Spirit convicts us of sin, never is the Holy Spirit identified as an accuser. God's way of confronting his people in their sin Paul calls "godly grief" (2 Cor. 7:9–11).

First, godly grief produces not just tears or new resolutions. It actually produces repentance—which means a real turning point. The change is tender; it is new and incomplete, but it is real.

Second, the grief from God leads the person back to a fresh acquaintance with the provision of salvation—the merit and mercy of Jesus. His sandals, the cross, the empty tomb, his present intercession and advocacy—these form a glad reunion in the person's being. The person knows that ultimately it is God he has sinned against and God for whom he comes home.

Third, grief from God purposes to send regret away: "For godly grief produces a repentance that leads to salvation without regret" (2 Cor. 7:10).

In contrast, there is a kind of sorrow for sin that has nothing to do with God. Over the years I have found that those caught in the sin of lying, for example, require the most active energy and time—particularly if lying has been a way of life.

Why is this so? On the one hand, a long life of this sin gives a person a very strong skill set with manipulation. Such a person is adept at tears, quoting the right verses, giving meaningful looks of the eyes, and saying what the person in front of him wants to hear. It is easy to conclude that someone has godly grief when actually he is feeling sorrow because he got caught and is simply trying to do what he needs to in order to get everyone off his case and to get back to normal.

On the other hand, when grace begins teaching a liar how to tie his shoes again, as with any other sin and sinner the change often does not come all at once but in fits and starts. This means that the liar requires time to begin to see how deeply she lies and how thoroughly words of spin saturate her daily life. For this reason, a person whom Jesus is actually changing will tell the truth in the same conversation that undetected lies are also present. It is easy to conclude then that a liar isn't actually changing at all, when, in fact, a powerful change is taking place. It just takes much more time than we want.

In light of all this, the point Paul makes has been invaluable. A grief that is self-generated and made mischief with by the Devil "produces death," Paul says (v. 10). That is, it sheds tears but does not turn; it makes resolutions and quotes verses. But it neither rests upon Jesus alone nor surrenders to God.

Regret still tells the story in the first-person present, as if we are still in the moment. It happened years ago, but we who listen get the idea from you that it happened recently.

Regret can also keep secrets. We put the lid on it and tell no one in order to preserve our image. It gradually eats away at us. But godly grief will eventually turn our sinful secrets into testimonies of grace.

Where Do We Start?

In Galatians 6 Paul says, "If anyone is caught in any transgression" (v. 1). By "anyone," Paul refers in context to those who profess to follow Jesus. He expounds on this elsewhere:

> I wrote to you in my letter not to associate with sexually im-
> moral people—not at all meaning the sexually immoral of this
> world, or the greedy and swindlers, or idolaters, since then you
> would need to go out of the world. But now I am writing to you
> not to associate with anyone who bears the name of brother if
> he is guilty. . . . For what have I to do with judging outsiders?
> Is it not those inside the church whom you are to judge? God

judges those outside. "Purge the evil person from among you."
(1 Cor. 5:9–13)

First, according to Paul, our task is not to separate from and judge
our non-Christian neighbors. To do so we'd have to leave the world
(a lot of us get this terribly wrong).

Second, when Paul says, "in *any* transgression," our hearts are
searched, for he includes any kind of stained thing that we might
come across in someone's closet.

Prior to vocational ministry I worked with victims of crime
in Blackford County, Indiana. I was unprepared for the kinds of
transgressions that existed outside my window. The job pulled back
the curtains of the world—murder, molestation, domestic violence,
child abuse, drug use. In the pastoral ministry, the fact that these
issues take place in churches too has often caught me off guard.
A youth pastor who has sex with girls in the youth group, a man
who fabricates the death of his son to his coworkers, a woman
who bankrupts her family through habitually lying about and ma-
nipulating bank funds. Paul's words, "any transgression," get our
attention and locate our pastoral work.

Third, Paul clarifies that entering the mess of a caught sinner's
recovery is off-limits to most of us. How different! In my church
experience, many people take it upon themselves and believe it their
role and business to confront whatever they see in whomever they
see it. But Paul says otherwise. Only those "who are spiritual should
restore him" (Gal. 6:1).

By "spiritual," Paul references the context of the previous verses
with which he addressed the fruit of the Spirit in contrast to the
works of the flesh. If we intend to confront or find ourselves confronting a caught sinner by using the tools of enmity or strife or fits
of anger, for example, then we are not the ones to walk with the
caught sinner. Someone else who is "spiritual," that is, given the
grace to engage the sinner with love, peace, patience, kindness, and
self-control, has this job, for such a sinner must be restored "in a
spirit of gentleness" (v. 1).

Furthermore, it is a transgression or a sin we are talking about. Church discipline (as with any kind of discipline, such as that of parents with kids) has to do with sins. This means we have no cause to discipline because someone differs in opinion with us, has a different style of teaching, expresses a different temperament than we do, or doesn't do what we want him to do or do it when we think he should.

Not every weakness or struggle arises from sin. Imagine a parent with a child who spills milk. Sin is not the only possible cause of the spilled milk, and therefore the parent may have no warrant for treating the child as if he is in trouble. To begin, children (and adults) have limits. A two-year-old cannot do what a five-year-old can. A child has to be five before he can be ten. Just as we do not discipline a first-grader if she gets a fifth-grade math problem wrong, so a two-year-old may spill milk because his hands and coordination are not yet what they will be.

Children not only have limits; they also have accidents. A child may have simply tried to pass the peas, and without intent or malice, knocked over the milk. In such a case, our frustration is our own issue to take to the Lord and not something we can legitimately discipline our child about. Accidents can have greater consequences when they involve swinging a baseball bat or driving a car. A teen driver who, while driving the speed limit, does not see the toddler run out from behind a parked car has to face the nightmare of a situation he didn't choose. Those who care for him maintain for his conscience that there is a difference between him and the one who tries to drive recklessly or even premeditates harm to a child.

Further nuance reminds us that, for adults, accidents can also stem from blind spots, particularly in relationships. Church small groups and ministry teams often encounter this.

> Like a madman who throws firebrands, arrows, and death
> is the man who deceives his neighbor
>   and says, "I am only joking!" (Prov. 26:18–19)

Often, adults will inflict pain on others by their relational words or actions and act surprised that another is hurt. Adults respond to the hurt they caused with, "I meant nothing by it," or, "That was not my intent," or, "I was just kidding." This is true. They did not actively intend the hurt. Often, therefore, they assume the problem lies with the one who feels hurt. "She shouldn't feel that way; she has a problem," and the adult moves on. The "accident" is actually a sin due not to intention but to lack of instruction.

The problem is that such adults are blind to the impact of their way of relating because they have neither seen nor learned the folly of what they are doing. So without meaning to, hurt is caused nonetheless. While sometimes it is true that the offended one can learn to grow less sensitive, it is equally true that saying, "I didn't mean anything by it," can act as an excuse. Help comes when these adults let the unintended wound transition from an excuse to a red flag. Constantly causing unintended harm invites the adult to pull off to the side of the road and take a fresh look at how he is driving. Perhaps a change by grace is in order.

A sin differs from a limit or an accident in exactly this: if the child holds up the glass and bold-faced glares at the parent, the parent says no (assuming the child has learned what this word means), and the child drops the glass and not the glare, now we are in the realm of a sin. And yet even here Paul teaches us that the wrong done does not justify our borrowing the works of the flesh in order to discipline the wrongdoer.

By the way, an individual leader might not have the grace to enter a particular sinner's plight (a molested person with a molester, a battered woman with an abuser), but as a whole, the Jesus community is meant to have the capacity to do so. A question arises: Is there any kind of sin that we would find ourselves unwilling to enter or unable to treat in a Jesus way? Our answer will show us where we need individual grace and a community in Jesus that can handle more things collectively than we can personally.

Conclusion

I often think about Judas and Peter.

Both sinned terribly. Both wept bitterly.

Worldly and godly grief are put on display and set in contrast.

One grieved his wrong but did not turn. His was no depression, no diseased fit from chemical mismanagement. This was different. He hanged to his own solution for his sin. Regret, no salvation, the two hands that tied the rope.

The other man found more than weeping—splashed in the prayer and intercession of a Savior. Every day the rest of his life, roosters still crowed. They didn't leave Jerusalem. Every day the foul reminders still screeched, and Peter heard them. But the cross stands. The tomb empties. The regret fades. The character grows. The crow fades. God holds the man.

14

Local Knowledge

How did we come here to this broken wood? Can we build a house here, make friends with the mangled stumps?

EDWIN MUIR

God has arranged it. To open his book necessarily requires an act of love for unknown neighbors and places. To access him, we have to read pages of stories about people whose names we cannot pronounce from places we've never heard of. To know him, we have to do context and background into the specifics of mundane life among people who at first glance are irrelevant to us. Think about that for a moment, won't you? After all, you are an unknown person in an unknown place who will seem irrelevant to most people in the world today, not to mention those who will read about your life centuries from now. And yet God gathers up every detail of your days with love and interest. The next time you open his book, remember this local knowledge that God wants you to inhabit, okay?

Calling
Most of us, in our ordinary places, intend, when we say that God has called us, that over a period of time we'd grown locally attentive

to an inward desire that ebbed and flowed but didn't fade. We then set this desire prayerfully before God moment by moment, day by day. We took steps during that time to test by Scripture in community whether we had the gifts to match this desire. Along the way, those who locally knew us best and those whom we'd attempted to serve told us that they were strengthened in Jesus because of our use of these gifts. Consequently, after a time (years maybe), we took awkward and frightening steps of faith, not knowing where these steps might lead. But by then we were assured by this unfading desire and these community affirmations in the context of God's Word that God might actually be leading us. Circumstantial opportunities then arrived, and we surrendered our lives toward these givens out of obedience and gratitude to God.

What I've just described sounds like a crash course in the slow, ordinary listening learned from the poor wise man or the beholding suffering servant, doesn't it?

My question for you is this: What if this way that God uses to call most of us to ministry is itself an education in the kind of skills the ministry requires?

Yet a strange thing happens to us. Once we become pastors, many of us leave off with this kind of listening altogether. Instead, we react, talk a lot, and constantly present ourselves as individuals with expertise and experiences who already know what is needed and can quickly take action in order to solve any question or problem presented. This is no more apparent than when we try to assert our vision and change the culture of a congregation. This is a problem.

Explorers and Road Builders

Early Arctic explorers made this same crucial error. They excitedly envisioned the place and came to it fortified by their own cultural assumptions. The result? They died. They were found frozen in the ice with their volumes of books and fine dishes, wearing coats unwisely tailored to handle the winters they'd always known.

Others fared better. These explorers acted as if the Arctic had a storyline of conditions, people, and places that preceded them. They slowed down, studied the terrain, listened, and learned from the people who lived there. These explorers lived.

Paying attention to "native technology," a knowledge local to the place, forged the differing fates of these two expeditions. While the first group brought horses that could not survive the climate, the second group thought to ask questions such as why it was that natives didn't use horses but relied on dogs instead.[1]

A similar analogy arises between path makers and road builders. Whereas our first story exposes the damage that visionary explorers can do to themselves, this story reminds us of damage that visionary explorers can do to the places they come to.

Path makers in early America created ways of travel that attempted to keep the place that preceded it intact. Road builders, in contrast, used dynamite to blast anything out of its preferred direction. Compelling to this history is an observation. Path makers often inhabited the place itself, while road builders often had no intricate knowledge of or long commitment to it.

> Because they belonged to no place, it was almost inevitable that they should behave violently toward the places they came to.[2]

What both stories highlight is a tendency to assert our vision for a place without having known it or loved it first. In both cases unnecessary damage occurs. When pastors do this with congregations (or vice versa), the damage is done in God's name.

Too Early to Tell

In 1 Kings 12 Rehoboam becomes king and immediately desires to assert his vision for the people of the land. The people express their fatigue. They recount for Rehoboam the conditions and stories of what life has been like for them. They ask for a slower pace than what he intends.

Rehoboam turns for advice to two differing groups—one young

and one old. The old ones advise Rehoboam to listen to the people. If he will know them and wait for their sake in the short run, the people, having felt heard and understood, will wholeheartedly follow him in the long run. In contrast, the young ones advise that Rehoboam as king does not have to listen to the people. On the contrary, Rehoboam must demonstrate his power and demand their allegiance and work.

By now, we might say, these young ones had not heard of the poor wise man. They could not imagine that patient listening, learning, and attending could serve as a true act of kingly power, that such a humble and listening posture could pave the way for clear vision wisely carried out over a long period of time.

Rehoboam overlooked the slow pace of the wise. He listened to folly. The kingdom divided against him and ultimately itself (1 Kings 12:1–16).

It is not uncommon to hear pastors complain in their opening chapters of ministry in a new place. "People don't follow me," we say. "They don't share my vision." "I've laid out the plan God gave me, set clear directives, and put in well-designed structures, but all I have is division and pain on one side and apathy on the other. Maybe it's time for me to leave." We say all this, and we've been there only eighteen months or twenty-nine.

It might be time to leave, but I'm learning to say that in most cases, it is too early to tell. Particularly if we've tried to import our own vision without attending to native technology, or if we've used dynamite as a leadership style to blast holes to push our vision roads through.

Take note of this if you can. Most of the time, a congregation and pastor are not troubled by one another in terms of their common purpose to see people changed by the gospel. The problem often has more to do with cultural assumptions that both the congregation and we as pastors bring to this common purpose. Consequently, two years into the work we hurt and are frustrated. *I just wanted to see individual lives changed for Jesus,* we think to ourselves. *Why then are some people upset because I moved the prayer meeting to Saturday mornings? And why is that elder bothered so much with me? I can't think of anything I said or did to offend him. And what is the big deal anyway that I don't use bullet points in my deacons' meeting agenda or that I don't use PowerPoint slides when I'm preaching? And why are seasoned Christian people bothered that during my sermon I'm helping non-Christian visitors know how to locate the sermon text in the Bible? Oh, and where did people get the idea that I don't care about our nursery volunteers, and who cares that I didn't wear a tie last Sunday?*

Mark this down. When you pastor a congregation, you not only cultivate the spiritual formation of a people but also the cultural formation of a place.

Humbling Ourselves

Eighteen months after I preached barefoot on that auditorium floor of second chances, many in our congregation were no longer impressed. So on a Sunday morning (the same week I was leading a conference on preaching in another state), I asked everyone listening in my congregation what I never imagined saying to them: "Will you teach me to preach? I need your help."

People were leaving our congregation in droves for many reasons, and my preaching was one of them. I had three choices. Quit, tantrum with authority (as Rehoboam's young counselors had advised), or humble myself into listening for local knowledge.

I wanted to quit and tantrum. But sometimes trusting Jesus will mean that you and I must do what we would rather not so that those we serve can see what they must of him (John 21:18).

So I humbled myself, and we established several open houses. People came and told me all the ways that I could preach better. In my pride I'd cry to God, "They'd be rightly offended if I walked into their office having no training or experience in what they do and told them how to do their job better." Then I'd bellow more to

God. "I don't deserve this. A few of these folks even seem to want to hurt me. They don't want to love me. They want me to produce the experience they want, or they'll go elsewhere."

The consumer threat of "going elsewhere." Sometimes shepherds wish they could make the same threat. But then the wolves would come, and what good would that do?

Finally, the gentle graces would come like the soft rains, reminding me in the night watches of my tears that I am not a businessman but a shepherd, not a hireling but a pastor given the task of spiritual care of a people loved by God. My life is not my own. Neither is yours.

So what texts are there that can teach us about making paths conducive to what is native rather than dynamiting our way through a congregation with our vision?

Titus

Crete was a start-up church in need of real help and difficult labor. It was out of the way, without prestige and without reputation, except that it was notoriously corrupt. But there was a story brewing in Crete. Jesus has something to say there. What is a great man with superior gifts like Titus supposed to do for Jesus when he gets there? Paul tells us.

Get to know local and ordinary persons and begin to disciple those who are gifted to lead ("appoint elders," Titus 1:5). Titus is to learn the names and stories of local people.

Spend time getting to know each local town and seek its welfare in this way ("in every town," v. 5). Titus is to learn the names, conditions, and needs of local towns in his region.

Become savvy to local narratives that oppose the gospel ("There are many who . . . must be silenced," vv. 10–11). Titus must spend time learning the local teachings, assumptions, and personalities that challenge the gospel.

Spend time getting to know local families for their pastoral care ("They are upsetting whole families," v. 11). Titus is to equip families to walk with Jesus amid these local challenges.

Become familiar with the history and literature of the place ("One of the Cretans, a prophet [poet] of their own, said . . . ," v. 12). Titus needs to read the news and local spokespersons.

Cultivate a congregational culture that is relational in its ethos (older men, younger men, older women, younger women, 2:1–6). Titus is to care about the formation of a relational environment in which they do life together.

None of this can happen in a day.

Here are some things to slow down and grow attentive to before you light a fuse or bring your handheld organ to the tundra.

Words and Memories

First, remember that this culture and these people existed before you arrived. They've already used words and given meanings to them, something we all do.

Mention the word *Mamaw* to me, and my memory awakens. I hear her voice saying, "My lands," or, "He's a dandy," or referring to me as "Charlie Brown." I see her watching travel shows on television, wearing yellow short sleeves, walking in the yard picking up sticks, or sitting quietly with the unspoken meaning that sometimes danced and sometimes cried in her eyes at Christmas. I smell her perfume or the effect of sweat on her skin from the hours she spent cooking green beans with bacon. I see the dirt under her fingernails from her garden digging that planted and harvested those same green beans. I smell the soap from the shower, the musty wood from the stairs that Papaw built. I taste her macaroni with tomatoes, the chick-a-sticks she brought me after work when I was a boy, and the tears I kissed on her cheeks before she died. I feel her embrace on the porch when heading back to college. I feel her dark hair dried and surrendered on her forehead in hospice. To mention the word *Mamaw* in a flippant way, or even a harmless way, is to enter my story and stir my emotional waters. My being wakens with sense.

When you say any word, such as *Mamaw, children, death, theology, Bible, evangelism,* or *grace,* you do so in a context of meanings that were established before you arrived. You might have to clarify what you mean for a while and learn what it is they mean. To do so isn't to face undo trial but to engage normative pastoral work.

Local Knowledge of Pastors

Second, this also means you are not the first pastor in someone's life in this place.

The positive experiences people have had with previous pastors will show up in their comments and memories. They will tell you the wonderful things the previous pastor(s) said or did and remind you (without malice and quite unconsciously) about how these other pastors would have handled something differently from you.

Those who have had painful experiences with pastors will feel nervous around you, though you have done or said nothing to offend or harm.

If you are married, and if you have children, you will hear that the previous pastor's wife did such and so. The children of the pastor two pastors ago were this or that.

In all this, we are prone to think that *calling* means we can say something and they will do it. Their lack of trust and regular comparisons, suspicions, or hesitations offend our pride. But trust takes time and faithfulness. It cannot be demanded by accepting a call or cajoled by credentials.

During this stage, so much of what people do not like about us has little to do with us and more to do with how they are trying to adjust to the other pastor's absence. We long for the day (in our better moments) when we will be critiqued because someone knows us. Out of love, they speak to us their question or concern on our own terms without attributing bad motives to us or bewailing our obvious (to them) lack of love for Jesus in comparison or contrast to this or that other person.

My point is that what I'm describing is typical to cultural change and not unique to you. Learning to grow attentive in order to navigate this terrain is normal pastoral work.

Local Memories of Time

I also have found it worthwhile to ask, "How many pastors have been here before me and how long did they stay?"

If previous pastors stayed three years on average, then many in your congregation have a clock in their mind (without even realizing it). They will hold back levels of trust because they assume that you too will go soon. As the third year approaches they might even feel jittery with you and not know why.

It is no surprise, then, that a core member of our congregation met me for coffee in the midst of my third year and asked me plainly (with humble kindness), "So, I'm thinking that you've been here for about three years now. I don't mean to pry, but many of us are grateful for you, and we've been kind of wondering if you are heading on to somewhere else, or if you are thinking you might take up the cause and join in with us for a while?"

Around the same time the elders and I went deeper together by accident. I figured that they were secretly hoping I might go. It turns out they thought I was probably going to tell them I was leaving (since I'd been there for over three years). We both discovered that neither of us wanted to leave the other. We laughed and cried. Since then we've trusted too.

As I write this, it's been almost four years since those conversations took place. Once people knew I was in it with them for a while (and I knew it in reverse), a lot changed. Trust deepened. So did our next season of life and ministry together.

Local Leadership Culture

Third, someone led before you got there. These persons aren't necessarily titled; you know who they are because when a decision in a meeting must be made, they are the ones whose voices people wait for. The congregation waits for these leadership voices because of a long history of wisdom found there. You won't know these leaders unless you've taken time to get to know people. Most likely, such quiet leaders can prove helpful as you get to know and learn from one another and seek the welfare of the congregation. Without this kind of attentive care, some of us never realize that we dynamited this kind of leader out of the way when we first arrived in order to push our vision through.

But at other times congregations wait for these leadership voices because they are afraid and tired. They know that to disagree is to bring conflict into their lives. So, long ago, they all learned to be quiet and bear with it. A culture develops in which the people tread lightly with this leader, who may blindly think it is because he is wise and strong. Such persons know what they are doing, and they keep doing it because it works. They get their way.

Over time, the congregation waits to see how you will respond to this frightening leader. If you begin to gently but firmly teach and redirect him, you will find that other people who've been mistreated begin to feel defended for the first time in years.

Some will start to help. But others might feel afraid that you won't stay. If you confront him and they join you but then you leave early, they are left out on a limb. But as people see that you are faithfully intentional, they will learn from you and follow. In addition, quite apart from this frightening leader, you continue to invest in the congregation as a whole. People begin to give thanks for your leadership and what they are learning from you. As this gradually happens, the frightening leader is actually being offered a gospel opportunity. Maybe for the first time in years he is being invited to change and grow. He will have to decide in time whether to surrender to that invitation or to harden and fight. I've seen it go both ways. The first way is incredibly beautiful. The second way isn't.

In all this, don't underestimate two truisms. (1) More often than not, the primary leader who brought you to the church as your greatest advocate in the beginning will fight you in the end. A leader with that kind of influence will not easily give it away when you arrive. (2) The differences in personality between you and the previous pastor or leaders wreaks more havoc than you know. If the previous pastor was an introverted poet who used metaphors for six years, and you come along with extroverted bullet points, crisp prose, and lists, everyone (at least in a consumer-oriented culture) has to adjust.

Local Theological Culture

Fourth, remember that prior to your arrival people had theological cultures through which they heard the world. One way to think of this is through a rubric called the Waltz of the Gospel.[3] Adapted for my local purposes, it speaks of three movements in the gospel life:

- confessing our mess (sinning and being sinned against),
- receiving Christ's love (turning to Jesus as forgiven and dearly loved children),
- walking his paths (conforming our lives to obediently following Jesus).

These three movements are often broken somehow in our lives. Congregations will have varying two-step emphases prior to your arrival:

- Some are trying to confess and walk without receiving. These folks work hard. They frown on grace, joy, and rest. When you talk of grace, they get concerned about you.

- Some are trying to receive and walk without confessing. These folks stay strong. They frown on appearing needy for forgiveness or imperfect. So when you talk about humility, sharing burdens, feeling emotions, and not trying to keep up appearances, they get concerned about you.

- Some are trying to confess and receive without walking. These folks want to relax. They frown on obedience. When you talk about the change in direction that Jesus's grace makes upon our actions and way of life, they get concerned about you.

Identify the kinds of concerns that people express, and you receive clues about the area of teaching and pastoral care they need and why their cultural differences with you are causing conflict. Begin to listen. If people are concerned about grace or unhidden brokenness or obedience, ask why. Where did this come from in their local history? What are they afraid will happen? How has it been misused in their lives? What kind of teaching have they had on these issues?

Another rubric for helping you listen is the three omni-temptations that we've already talked about. Grow attentive to this question: Do the ways of being and doing in this congregation praise you or your leaders most when you appear to know it all (relate to them as an expert with answers), fix it all (have power and ability with solutions), or be everywhere for everybody (always accessible)? On which of these do you or other leaders receive the most criticism: expertise, solutions, or accessibility?

Listening in these gospel-waltz and omni-temptation ways takes lots of attentive time. Two things will emerge though. (1) You will begin to have pastoral wisdom regarding what to teach and when, in your sermons and Bible studies, so as to compassionately and wisely help the church grow as the Scriptures point them to Jesus. (2) You can begin to affirm what frightens or concerns them about such and so and then lead them from there to what the Scriptures affirm about such and so in order to deliver them from their fears and concerns.

Added to this is a further question: What theological culture of evangelism and outreach has been cultivated in this congregation? What barriers to the gospel does this congregation unwittingly put up that make it hard for non-Christians to hear about and grow in Jesus?

In our context I began to realize that many people come to our congregation with real suspicion, pain, and cynicism regarding churches, but they are compelled by the person of Jesus. I began to adapt my teaching in this direction. Instead of doing a class or sermon series on systematic theology, we focused instead on what Jesus believes about the Bible, about God, about himself, about the world, about sin, about churches, and about the afterlife. We still focus there. We access other doctrines explicitly through the centrality of how Jesus speaks of them. It turns out that this approach helps Christians too, not only for themselves, but in learning how to share these other doctrines in a way that neighbors can make sense of.

A shift like this, born slowly out of local knowledge and then taught before enacted, can nonetheless cause know-it-alls, for example, to fidget. They want to hear us use theological language more historic to our heritage (even though they themselves didn't learn this language until years along in their walk with Jesus). They forget this and expect people to begin their walk with Jesus at the point where they themselves have arrived. Mostly, they fear a culture change in which they have to learn theology through an explicit Jesus lens. The unknown makes them hesitant and suspicious that we might be growing liberal. Those who try to receive and walk without confessing their mess grow nervous with the thought that openly broken people might start to frequent the church more often.

Hearing God's Call

With all this, let's remind ourselves of two important realizations about entering the culture of a congregation.

First, we all know that ideally a pastor is a change agent in God's hands for the good of a congregation. As a seasoned pastor, I have tried to work hard and faithfully at this side of our vocation. But I've been learning something equally if not more important and rarely cherished among us clergy. I've been learning that a congregation is a change agent in God's hands for the good of a pastor too. Failing to recognize the role of the congregation in the pastor's spiritual formation and in a community's gospel transformation negatively alters how we view what a pastor is supposed to be and do. God uses a congregation and its neighbors to show you things about him that you would not see otherwise. In other words, pastor, congregational life is not primarily about you. God precedes you both.

Second, God sometimes calls us to a congregation when we don't yet have what it needs. Sometimes we can't help a people until after we've been with them for a while, and being with them is the means God uses to teach us what he wants us to offer them. For some reason, how we handle our painful incapability with Jesus day upon day becomes formative for those who stick it out with us. How they stick it out with our incapable selves becomes formative for us too. Gradually, what we both have to offer, why God has knit us together, and why we need each other emerges.

In all this, what if the things we have to teach each other can't take shape unless we first confess the things we have to learn from each other? A congregation needs what a pastor brings to them— core and essential provisions such as prayer, spiritual direction, pastoral care, leadership, and the ministry of the Word. But sometimes a pastor won't know how God wants him to apply and live these core provisions until he has bumbled along in the presence of his congregation for a while, growing attentive to what God has been doing there long before he ever arrived.

Interview

We sat at a living room table. Our dinner plates had been cleared, and we were enjoying dessert. I was being interviewed. I'd been around long enough to know the two big questions that American church search committees want to know. I'd already answered the first one and felt sure that I hadn't done so in a satisfactory way. That one, of course, was, "What is your vision for this church?"

Years ago, for my first pastorate, I had answered that question with a five-point statement that included a prepared diagram that I handed out to everyone. "It was impressive," they said back then, and apparently so was I. But all these years later, with so many mistakes made, I no longer trusted as wisdom that after spending a total of four days over three months with people I had never met before, I knew what they needed from God. I used to think that way. But that was before I thought about shepherds and poor wise men, silences not just sentences, and the beholding work of the suffering servant.

So this time around my vision-for-the-church answer was, "I don't know. I have a handful of thoughts about what it means to love God and our neighbor and how that impacts what any congregation that follows Jesus will envision. I think Acts 2 offers us a helpful direction for the kinds of ministry that any congregation is meant to pursue. I know some truisms about Saint Louis, having lived here for a while, that might prove helpful. But as to how these biblical directives should take shape here in this particular congregation and community, I can't fully answer yet. We would need a lot more time together."

By the follow-up looks and questions I had received from these kind folks, it was obvious that I had answered strangely. So when the second imminent question arrived, I felt that I had nothing to lose: "Why should we call you to be our pastor?"

"I don't know for sure. I'm not yet certain that you should," I answered.

Each member looked at one another and then back at me. With a warm smile, one member responded, "I don't think that's the way you are supposed to answer that question." We all laughed a bit.

"I know," I said. "I know how I'm supposed to answer, and I can if you want. I can tell you my résumé, my stature, my years of experience and books, and my vision for why I can do for this church what no one else really can. Then I can tell you that God laid this or that on my heart and tell you that for his glory I believe we can mobilize and accomplish great things for a remarkable future."

"And there is a problem with that?" one of the members asked as she laughed kindly and leaned forward.

"Yes," I nodded. "If we can just be honest with one another, we all know that we've spent only a few hours together. They've been great, but we don't know each other well. You want a pastor, and I want a job. We are all putting our best foot forward. But one year from now, it won't matter much what great things we talked about here tonight. By then you will know my weaknesses, wounds, and sins, and I will know yours. What will matter one year from now is whether we will actually love one another with our strengths and weaknesses, hurts and sins. If not, our vision statements and plans won't come to fruition anyway, no matter how exciting or well worded. So I don't know how to do it, but I wish there was a way to get to this harder but truer question."

I look back, and I'm humbled. I wasn't trying to be coy or difficult. But I'm sure it was not easy for them. There were better ways to say this stuff, and I can see now that I was more cynical and hurt than I wanted to be. But being as honest as I knew how was my heart. I didn't want to pretend together, whether I would be their pastor or not. Whatever our grand plans, there was still a culture of doing life together that we'd have to contend with. I didn't want to hurt them or get hurt by them because we hadn't accounted for it. Somehow, in my imperfections, these dear folks graciously saw all that and knew it. We must have been made to be together. We've been so ever since. There is grace upon grace.

15

Leadership

But you must understand, there are many ways of being
in a place.

TERESA OF AVILA

You and I have learned many ways of being in leadership and not
all of them from Jesus. What if leading is mostly about trying to
embody what you invite others to follow?

Leading an Elders' Meeting

How do we learn to lead meetings in ways that help us relinquish
and resist the temptations we face? I can describe for you what five
years of listening has led us to. But this is no formula. Local knowledge will lead you to different details and strategies. But perhaps
what we are learning can give you a place to start.

After we've gathered, talked, weathered awkward silences,
laughed, listened to one another, and shared a scene or two from
each other's week, I invite us to pray. This is our monthly elders'
meeting. We are learning to shape it in light of what we've been
looking at in this book. So I'll say something like: "As we begin,
let's remind ourselves that a church meeting and a business meeting

are apples and oranges. They both have their important roles, but they represent two differing things."

Then I begin to read through the first portion of our stated agenda, something we do every month to begin each meeting. I often feel nervous that I'm being redundant. But these leaders remind me that they need this redundancy. It strikes them as so foreign to the air they breathe at work. So, I read on:

What we do: We shepherd the people of Riverside Church with our prayer, presence, teaching, and planning.

The next statement reads:

Our decision making: ER (immediacy and relief), BR (efficiency, quantity, and money) and Shepherding.

We remind ourselves that "Emergency Room" decision making relies upon immediacy and relief. "Board Room" decision making highlights efficiency, quantity, and money. At times elders need one or the other but neither as our norm. Most of the time the growth Jesus leads us into does not come immediately, doesn't necessarily relieve us, and is not very efficient.

Then we read 1 Peter 5:1–5, which is printed on the page: "Shepherd the flock of God that is among you . . ."

After we read it, I ask: "What sticks out to you from this verse tonight?" After a good, long pause, someone says, "Not for shameful gain."

For the next few minutes we share with one another the temptation to use our work as elders in such a way that we gain sinfully from the people we serve, like how holding a cup so that our member with cerebral palsy can drink from its straw can turn into a dark temptation to be seen by others for the way we care for people. We turn this conversation to prayer. Then I simply read down through the next section of bullet points. We remember:

- A church meeting is not a business meeting. We have a different bottom line.
- Our goal is not, as a norm, to do large things famously as fast as we can.
- No relationship is on the line tonight. We give each other the benefit of the doubt.
- Most of the time hurry will not help us.
- Building relationships and sharing our lives together is part of our agenda and is no waste of time.
- Oftentimes, we differ or disagree as a matter of temperament and perspective and not because one of us is sinning and the other one isn't.
- We are quick to give and to receive forgiveness when we do sin against each other.
- We seek to do our meetings the way elders are meant to do ministry.
- This thing we are doing is about Jesus, not us.

We are now thirty minutes into our meeting. We've shared stories, rehearsed our purpose, and searched our hearts briefly with God's Word.

Practicing at Game Speed

To practice at game speed is to run, catch, or kick the ball in practice at the same pace the game will require. But what if an elder's game speed requires us to slow down? After all, a shepherd is a returning one who is humanly limited but, like a poor wise man, meant to listen to someone else's story with patience, discernment, listening talk, and prayer. Why not try to cultivate a way of doing a meeting that practices the speed pastoral work calls for?

If every time we meet, we do reports and talk numbers for the sake of efficiency and relational guardedness, we end up practicing a way of meeting month upon month, year upon year. Three years into this way of doing a meeting, we've actually created a culture of leadership that relies on quantitative language, impatient pace, and impoverished relational skills. This culture differs dramatically from the actual language, pace, and skill that a congregational member will need most of the time from us as shepherds.

Therefore, next on our agenda we often read something related to ministry in real time and then talk about it. This resource time does two things. It allows us to engage in ongoing mentoring regarding our task. But it also requires us to slow down, listen to someone else read, and talk together about mattering things in hospitable ways.

When we first started doing this, it drove most of us restless. We felt strongly that we were wasting time. Perhaps in comparison to other kinds of business meetings, we were. But this kind of game speed enables us to practice what elders are supposed to become in the first place. This kind of practice also pays off when ER immediacy and relief suddenly storm crisis down into us, and we have to act quickly. We have a better shot at responding rather than reacting, because of the marathon stamina we've been working on.

After this sixty minutes of remembering, story sharing, praying, resource reading, and discussion, we move on to talking about pastoral care of ministries and persons, finances and planning. It isn't that we don't talk about numbers or programs. Rather, these two have to take their place farther back in line, surrounded by a relational context. This has taken painful and restless effort—lots of sorry saying, forgiving, second tries, and impatience. Detox and desert make their way in us for a while. Getting stripped of our cravings to quickly fix everything, know it all, and be everywhere all at once alters the habit of our inner life. Culture change takes time.

Training New Leaders

In this light, we've had to adjust the way we train new elders and other kinds of leaders. When I first started as a pastor, most of my largest mistakes had to do with leadership—my own, of course, but also my training of leaders. I just didn't know how. I would offer thirteen or sixteen classroom sessions emphasizing theology, highlighting the grand calling for which we are striving, and encouraging each one to prize his gifts and find a way that he can make a difference in our congregation. Unwittingly I played right into the know-it, fix-it, and be-everywhere cravings for fame that lurked within us. We paid a high cost for this. Elders were trained but not in the skills of their actual work, not as returning ones who are contemplative servants savvy with desert ways and able to sustain with a word him who is weary.

Every pastoral context differs. Each of us finds our ways and methods with the Lord where we are. But perhaps there is something here that might prove helpful to you. This is how we train now:

1. *Once a month for three months.* A candidate for elder meets with me once a month for three months.

2. *Teaching sessions.* When we meet, we talk for two hours about:

   - Session 1: What is an elder? (1 Tim. 3:1–7; Titus 1:5–9)
   - Session 2: What is love and the fruit of the Spirit? (1 Cor. 13:1–8; Gal. 5:16–26)
   - Session 3: What is the culture of our particular church? (History, purpose, leadership culture, strengths, and weaknesses—the assumptions I just outlined in the section above on leading a meeting)

3. *Homework conversations.* In between these sessions, the remaining month is meant for homework and thoughtful examination.

   - After discovering from the Bible what an elder is, the candidate asks his spouse (or closest friend, if unmarried), which one or two qualifications are already strong by grace and which ones are weaknesses, needy for grace in the candidate's life.
   - After discovering from the Bible what love is and what the fruit of the Spirit is, the candidate asks his spouse (or closest friend, if unmarried) the same questions.

- After discovering the culture of our church, the candidate asks his spouse (or closest friend, if unmarried), about his assumptions of the church. It is one thing to be qualified in general to serve as an elder. It is an equally important question as to whether one is willing and able to work peaceably and respectfully with a team and to work patiently with the strengths and weaknesses of the congregation, recognizing that God has preceded them. In this regard I ask an important question: "What would you change about our church if you could?" If the candidate answers, "I would change nothing; it is perfect!" it is possible that he is not yet ready to serve as an elder. At first glance he doesn't seem to know Riverside very well. Know us well enough, and our various needs for grace, growth, and change will be readily apparent. On the other hand, if the candidate offers a list of all things he would change, or changes he wants to make that strike at odds with the stated purpose and culture of the church, that candidate is possibly not ready. Working with our team out of love for what is graciously blessed or what requires time and patience might prove too difficult at the moment.

- The reason we ask candidates to talk with spouses in these ways is twofold. (1) It is important for an elder to be able to speak this intimately and nondefensively with his spouse. If this isn't possible, he probably is not ready to serve as an elder. (2) It is important that an elder can talk about personal strengths humbly and about personal needs for Jesus. An elder unable to speak transparently regarding his personal need for grace will make it difficult for people in the congregation who know themselves to be sinners to come and talk with him about it.

- Meanwhile, elder candidates read through the theological standards of our church (in our case, the Westminster Confession of Faith), keeping a notebook of questions.

After the three months, the candidate and I (or a current elder) will meet for extended lunch or coffee once or twice to go through the questions raised and highlighted content. This takes extra time, but the one-on-one interaction with theology over coffee offers an environment different from a group in a classroom. This can reveal a lot—not just about the theology itself as the candidate understands it—but also about how he actually talks about it. Being able to speak humbly and charitably about theology in a relational context, such as having coffee, is part and parcel of an elder's work.

4. *Interview.* In our fourth month, we invite the candidate who has completed his sessions and homework to an interview. I may or may not be in attendance. The interview is typically made up of two current elders and two current deacons. They ask questions in a welcoming and relational context regarding the candidate's sessions, homework, and conversations with his spouse (who is also at the interview). At no time is this process an interrogation. We are a family knit together in Jesus, prayerfully discerning together two things: (1) whether he is called to serve as an elder, and, if so, (2) if this is the right timing in light of his pace of life and other responsibilities.

5. *Asked to wait.* If cause for hesitation has bubbled up through the process, we ask the candidate to wait. We invite him to meet with me or another elder over the next year once a month to continue pursuing relationship together and to see what the Lord will show us. Usually at this point a candidate's character shows through in how he responds. If he is deeply offended, huffs and puffs, and leaves the church (assuming, of course, that we are gentle, full of love, and have issued a glad invitation to keep going once a month together), then perhaps the candidate wasn't ready, and the process has revealed it. Other candidates will respond with hurt pride but also with teachable hearts and humility. One or two years later, these folks are often serving as elders.

6. *Apprenticeship.* If a candidate is invited forward from the interview, the next phase is a six-month apprenticeship. He attends every elders' meeting, receives correspondence, quietly observes, and meets with me or another elder once a month for lunch to process what he is observing and learning about being an elder in general and on this team in particular. After six months, we present the candidate to the congregation for affirmation and approval. By this point, the candidate has trained for nearly one year.

Decision Making

How does our attempt to value small, mostly overlooked mattering things over long periods of time shape the way we attempt to make decisions as elders? To begin, I meet with each elder once a month for lunch, and we all try through fits and starts to find ways to spend time together in organic ways in the life of our church. We want to know each other well enough when no decisions are on the line so that when late-night crises arrive, we possess relational trust strong enough to handle moments in which any one of us may not be at our best.

Then we imperfectly move toward decision making with a framework of three questions found in Paul's words in 2 Timothy 2:23–26.

1) Is This the Right Thing?

Timothy must teach the Word and correct opponents. Yet, at the same time, he must "have nothing to do with foolish, ignorant controversies" (2 Tim. 2:23). How do leaders decide if a conflict arises from what God's Word says or from a misuse of God's Word to promote one's own agendas, speculations, or habitual commitments? An answer isn't easily discerned with haste.

Imagine a scenario that concerns the pastor's parking space. Some deacons argue that the pastor ought to park at the farthest distance from the church. Other deacons argue for spaces closest to the church. The disagreement adopts biblical tones.

One side argues that it is more biblical to park at a distance because pastors are to serve others and set an example. The other side states that it is more biblical for the pastor to park closer because honor belongs to those who lead. Though the Bible itself does not address where a pastor should park his car, both sides now believe they are fighting for truth in their church.

In the end, however, gospel ministry is stalled, leadership is divided, relationships are strained, and families leave because Christians disagreed about a parking space in the name of standing for truth in their generation.

Delegating the Dreaming

Along these lines, multiple decisions have little to do with biblical mandates. Worship bulletins, paint colors, fonts, carpets, meeting times, ministry styles, choirs, and parking lots are what I think of as "carpet decisions." Whether the carpet is this color or that should never divide a congregation or be used to hurt a congregational member in Jesus's name. This begins with the pastor and the elders. I've made too many mistakes here.

Consider what you think about this short scene. After worshiping in a school rental for twelve years, we bought an old church building in town. A young friend in ministry asked if I would walk him through the building and share with him my dreams for it. When I was a younger pastor I would have loved this! But the first thing I found myself saying now to my friend was that I had delegated most of the dreaming.

"What do you mean?" he asked. Then, looking at the empty sanctuary of scraped paint and scaffolding, he said, "Don't you want things in the sanctuary to look a certain way or to take a particular shape? What is your vision for it all?"

I laughed a bit and repeated what I'd try to say. "I've delegated most of that. Gifted people with expertise in various areas are leading multiple teams of volunteers who are doing the dreaming for the design of each area in the church."

In the pause, I realized that I needed to explain. "I don't mean that I've had nothing to say. I've given broad parameters in concert with the elders, but each team freely does what it is good at within those parameters. This means that I'm learning what the sanctuary will look like in terms of colors, placement of furniture, and design not much earlier than you are."

"But what if you don't like something that someone chooses?" he asked.

"Well, just about everybody in the congregation will not like something that someone chose. In that regard I'm no different from anybody. But I no longer believe that being the pastor means that God has favored my favorite color." I said this lightly with a bit of laughter.

"Why do you feel this way?" he asked. "That is different from the way I've thought pastors would handle these kinds of things."

I paused. I could see the seriousness of the questions. "Too much personality and power," I said. "If everyone is involved using their gifts, then the mark of the congregation as a whole, not of my individual personality, will undergird the place. This matters because someday in life I might not be here, but many of them will. Besides, many of these dear folks regard me in such a way that if I say I'd like something, they would make it happen. That is too much power about things that don't ultimately have much to do with the Bible at all."

"I don't understand how that works. It seems like that use of personality and power are part of leadership," he said.

"I get that. They are," I acknowledged. "But if I use it like that, in this moment I will likely forfeit my primary role as pastor, and that is what I actually want to be and am called to."

Another pause.

"I'm saying that if I have a stated opinion about the type of a chair, for example, or if I think it should sit in this place rather than that one, I am now on a side. When one gifted volunteer team thinks one way about the type and placement of the chair in contrast to the other volunteer team, I am no longer an honest broker able to shepherd these people. By my absence of worry about the chair within my larger concern for the overall vision and individual pastoral care of each member, I get to be their pastor, and we get to move through and on together."

I think back to that conversation, and my memory fills with stories from that time of ministry. Delegating the dreaming actually required multiple moving parts: equipped volunteers, constant communication, disagreements to work through, clarified processes, clarity of overall parameters, relational trust, and prayerful resistance to any temptation to take back what I said others could do. Besides all this, it was not always easy to resist my own color preferences or font placements, carpet colors, or HVAC details. But if a team of people all agree, and they actually do this sort of thing for a living, then I too get to become one who honors the gifts of others and surrenders my personal preferences for the sake of staying knit together and focused on the biblical goal in front of us.

The command to love one another and the belief that "God told me the church logo should be such and so" are simply not on the same plane.

2) What Is the Right Way to Do This?

We can also do the right thing in the wrong way. While Timothy teaches and corrects, he must be "kind to everyone" (2 Tim. 2:24), "with gentleness" (v. 25), and not "be quarrelsome" (v. 24). Paul says that the Lord's servant must not correct others with an attitude that is ready to pick a fight or rub another's nose in it. In other words, being right does not justify arrogance, intimidation, rudeness, or harshness. Holding the right position in the argument never justifies betraying the character of Jesus.

Imagine a scenario in which elders write a fifteen-page paper identifying why divorce is a sin. They include arguments from the Greek along with exhortations regarding the liberal slide of our culture. The elders send this paper to the congregation via mass e-mail, defining it as the official position of the church. The unintended result is widespread confusion, profound pain, and the fueling of self-righteousness, because while the paper states why divorce is a sin, it does not address how the gospel applies to those who are already divorced. The e-mail did not take into account the varying and sometimes tragic circumstances of those who were divorced in their congregation. There was no accounting for those who'd been abandoned for another, or who'd desperately done all they could to save the marriage, or who'd been physically endangered or misused.

Know-it-alls will almost always identify negative reactions to their decisions as the cost of standing for the truth and suffering for the Lord. But leaders may not realize that they can wrongly wound people with the right thing. Once we prayerfully determine the right thing to do, we must still contemplate the right way to do it.

Sometimes weak men use this appeal to gentleness and kindness to justify their passivity. Jesus, however, was far from passive. He actively pursued decision making. He disrupted evil. He exposed manipulative schemes and cultivated relational movement amid his fidelity to the Father's will. Gentleness does not equal or excuse passivity.

Conversely, others, in the name of leading strongly, resist postures of gentleness and kindness. Cultural norms and business environments often identify such fruit of the Spirit as weakness. Yet Jesus spoke directly without requiring an intimidating, harsh, or raging posture. This is true strength.

Still, some will say that gentleness and kindness are inefficient. Refraining from strong coercion slows things down. But perhaps God has already accounted for the slower pace and valued it. Still, even if God's way doesn't seem to work or seems to slow us down, the Lord's servants are required to lead differently from those who do not follow him.

3) Is This the Right Time?
Timothy must also patiently endure evil (2 Tim. 2:24). He must "reprove, rebuke, and exhort, with *complete patience*" (2 Tim. 4:2).

Consider a board of elders who comes to believe that it is right to rest from work on Sundays. Will the elders have the humility to recognize the long in-house debate about this subject among equally knowledgeable, committed, and genuine followers of Jesus?

Will they then seek the right way to introduce this view to the congregation with public and personal gentleness, kindness, and teaching? Now the question of timing arises. Several families have their kids in soccer leagues on Sundays. As members of the church, they have participated in these leagues for the last five years. Will the elders equip parents with the same amount of time and access to the same resources that they themselves needed in order to arrive at these convictions? Furthermore, will the elders help parents to remember that their older children may require equal amounts of time?

Someone will object that the thing is wrong and that it ought to stop immediately. But they do so forgetting what they themselves required from Jesus in order to know what is right. They also forget that there are many wrong things that need to stop. While God works with us on one sin, he bears with multitudes of others. He does this until the time when we can bear to hear from him on these other matters.

A know-it-all or fix-it-all makes a decision and expects immediate obedience, blind to the time she herself has needed to learn, and blind to the patience being extended to her in her many other mistakes and disobediences.

The Inner Ring

Along with decision making, I have found what C. S. Lewis called "the Inner Ring" to be the most difficult challenge to leadership. It tempts us to let go of "friends whom you really loved and who might have lasted a lifetime, in order to court the friendship of those who appear more important."[1]

What is an inner ring? "From outside, if you have despaired of getting into it, you call it, 'that gang' or 'they' or 'so-and-so and his set.'"[2] Deacons, elders, presbyters, boards, assemblies, donor bases, constituencies, committees, ministry teams, personalities, friendships, families—these function as inner rings. At their worst, local inner rings expose "our longing to enter them, our anguish when we are excluded, and the kind of pleasure we feel when we get in."[3]

The idol of the inner ring exposes why we are prone to excuse a fellow leader whom we love even though he or she is damaging others. We see this leader's dignity or gifts so plainly that when we experience pain or concern from darker sides of his character, we feel disoriented, find rationalizations, or get anxious about losing our relationship or our jobs or about upsetting others. The wisdom of being slow to judge one's weaknesses transitions into the folly of making a catalog of excuses.

I remember a man nominated as elder in one of the churches I served. Division arose among the other leaders as to whether this man was gifted to serve. Those who were cautious and thought it best to wait were outvoted. Two painful things surfaced almost immediately.

First, only weeks later, the elder cornered a church member after a congregational meeting, taking it upon himself to intensely correct the member for an answer given at the meeting. The parishioner, near tears and confused, shouted out to the pastor in the hallway for help.

Second, it came to light that no congregation members had actually nominated the man for leadership. Only his friends who were current elders had done so. Naïvely, these well-intentioned men, out of loyalty and love for a friend, usurped wise practice. They knew that no one in the congregation had yet recognized any gifts of shepherding in this person. But they excused that, because in their eyes the man was qualified, and they, after all, were the leaders. So they closed their eyes to the fact that he was untested with actual people and their care. The result is that the elder was defended (but not helped to grow) while the congregation was misused.

To slow down damage done by inner-ring leaders, Paul reminds Timothy, "Doing nothing from partiality. . . . Do not be hasty in the laying on of hands, nor take part in the sins of others. . . . The sins of some people are conspicuous . . . but the sins of others appear later" (1 Tim. 5:21–24).

On the other hand, a ministry leader can face the intimidation of a congregation with its various pockets of inner rings. Well-meaning friends can quickly pile on critiques of a leader. If one person in a close-knit small group begins to speak critically of a pastor, for example, the critique presses loyalties of the rest in the group. After recognizing a pattern of this kind of pastor critique, will they risk relationship with their friend by suggesting that the group is not the forum for tearing down the pastor, or that the all-or-nothing way of speaking about the pastor probably isn't accurate to who Jesus is in the pastor's life? Because of each one's desire to remain accepted by the inner ring, each will be tempted either to remain consistently silent or to join in.

To slow down the damage that inner rings within congregations can cause, Paul counsels Timothy, "Let the elders who rule well be considered worthy of double honor. . . . Do not admit a charge against an elder except on the evidence of two or three witnesses" (1 Tim. 5:17, 19).

Partiality to preserve the inner ring creates an organizational culture that defends what should be abandoned and abandons what should be defended and leaves both the abandoned and the defended without the gospel.

What will it mean for us to trust Jesus rather than our inner ring to save us? Such trust creates leaders of a different kind. The grace of it all breathes into us and sets us free.

16

Romantic Realism

Nothing is sweeter in this sad world than the sound of
someone you love calling your name.

KATE DiCamillo

Creatures in Eden,
craving.

This man, this woman, seen,
by shepherds, these

returning ones,
like poor wise men in small places,
forgotten by those they help to deliver,
but known by Him, whom they behold
in silences, listening, moment by moment
to sustain with a word,

a widow, a farmer, a pastor with a name and town,

our heroes, these
invisible followers
of the fame-shy.

Widows and Farmers

I know that the call of prophet and king sounds nobler than widow and farmer. After all, prophet and king signify grand positions for heroic moments in a generation. I do not disparage this. We long for a generation in which God would grant us such leaders. We take up Elijah on Mount Carmel, for example, and long that we too could stand against the false prophets and teachings of our age with such courage. And no wonder! For consider that in the days of the judges, when "everyone did what was right in his own eyes" (Judg. 21:25), God raised up men and women for mighty deeds and champion events (Judg. 2:16). Oh, to rise, like Deborah or Gideon or Samson, not with swords but with true spiritual power! We look at our times. We see everyone doing what is right in their own eyes. We, too, rightly long for such reformation and revival. Those of us prone to resignation need Jesus to reawaken such longings for our generation.

But those among us who are called to pastoral work more often need the farmer's and the widow's help. These unlikely heroes teach us some vital things about God and our vocation.

First, there are heroes who never receive the limelight of their generation. While the judges publicly participated in substantial cultural change, a farmer named Boaz quietly walked the muddy fields, planted grain, fairly treated his workers, and sought the common good of his community with ordinary, daily, prayerful, and hard work. This farmer loved a Gentile woman and her family. They made an ordinary life of real love together. They loved God. Those who know the story will argue that this ordinary love and life proved equal to if not greater than the mighty deeds of the judges in that generation.

Second, heroic moments are heavenly but not heaven. What relief, what celebration, what gratitude and happiness arise when a people is delivered from oppression, corruption, and foul treatment; when souls are awakened; when dignity and integrity and decency form again not just the slogans but the actions of a land! And yet the effects of heroic moments fade. This was true in the times of the judges. The human heart was not intrinsically changed in a universal way by mighty deeds. In a matter of time, another generation would need another judge. And even these powerful deliverances could not bring back Naomi's family or Ruth's husband. The revivals came but the gravestones still remained in Moab.

Third, sometimes visitations from God are discovered when ordinary bread is placed on the table of an ordinary family (Ruth 1:6). Sometimes the aid of God is found in the provision of a mundane grain or an ordinary friend.

Fourth, heroic moments have as their aim the recovery of the ordinary. Deborah and Gideon are raised up by God so that everyone can return home to do life in peace. The great triumph of a fictional Superman is to free the citizens of Metropolis from evil so that they can go back to work, and marry, and live, and eat, and find meaning. The great triumph of the Greatest Generation was to free the world from tyranny so that people could go back to the blessing and joy of daily life and love. The true act of heroism in Jesus on the cross and the emptying of the tomb is so that his people can return to the grace of doing life with God in a place, with love for our neighbors, and the freedom to enjoy God in the work, play, rest, and love that he gives us there.

Romanticism and Resignation

Without these remembrances, some of us are burning ourselves out with romanticism. We cannot find God in the ordinary. We restlessly move ourselves from one grand moment to the next. We regularly push others into the same whirlwind. We have little room in our ministry for a Naomi who does not get her husband back or a locality in which the grand visitation from God is that ordinary supper tables have food again. We have trouble seeing how it is glorifying to God to eat food, learn to love, go to bed, and get up the next day for the same old work. The thought of living and ministering in one or two unknown and ordinary places for fifty years and then going home to be with the Lord feels like death. Of what account to God is an ordinary life in the grain fields?

Others of us inwardly decay through resignation. We too cannot find God in the ordinary, but we have long given up on anything extraordinary being given by God or accomplished through us. "Call me Mara," we say with Naomi (Ruth 1:20). No love will ever find Ruth again. No bread will come to our table. No judge will save us. All is bitter and with little point in trying. I think my pastor friend who took his life must have landed here. Of what account to God is an ordinary life in the grain fields?

The result is an "all or nothing" kind of thinking. Either everything is grand or nothing is—and either way, a grain field isn't grand enough (e.g., Adam and Eve with Eden). Romanticism and resignation both have this motto in common.

In contrast to both, Jesus calls us to a romantic realism. He purchased this for us on the cross. We long for heroic moments but recognize that they aren't heaven and that someone else among a rare few will most likely have that momentary role. We are realistic about the fact that heroic moments are not the normal way that God daily visits his people. And yet we still believe that God is doing something larger than we can presently see. Out of his love for us, he is recovering in Jesus what was lost. We are realistically romantic. We see bread on a table and give thanks to God! Bread isn't just bread anymore. Bread is a gift—God has remembered us. Ordinary love the way it is meant to be, along with a long life of ordinary faithfulness to God, accomplishes more than we know. A farmer, a widow, and a Gentile in an unknown place all their lives may actually reveal in the end the true greatness of God. A romantic realist talks like this:

> If you were to rank the most important people in the generation of the judges, who would they be? Gideon? Deborah? Samson? What mighty deeds! What help God brought through them. But Jesus purchased new eyes to see more than the heroic. Matthew, in the first Gospel of the New Testament, tells us of two others

who likewise lived during the times of those awesome judges. He records for us "the book of the genealogy of Jesus Christ, the son of David, the son of Abraham" (1:1). In verses 5 and 6, Matthew says this: ". . . Boaz the father of Obed by Ruth, and Obed the father of Jesse, and Jesse the father of David the king."

While everyone did what was right in his own eyes and reformers sought powerfully to turn the spiritual tide, the promise of Genesis 3:15 was being pursued by God on a mundane farm amid the shattered and recovered dreams of ordinary love and life.

The romanticized and the resigned—neither would have seen Ruth, the royal lady in the line of the King. While the romanticized stood in line to get the autograph of someone like Gideon, and while the resigned stayed home and complained about the hype, neither would have noticed the tremendous movement of God in their midst.

No matter how great or gifted we are, God invites us to himself for the sake of local people in a local place with the long learning of local knowledge in Jesus until he comes. This means that if you are wearing yourselves out trying to be and do more than this, Jesus is calling you to stop all this tramping about and come finally home. The great work to be done is right in front of you with the persons and places that his providence has granted you. For me, this means reading the *Webster-Kirkwood Times* or the *St. Louis Post Dispatch*, when it sounds much more sexy and feels much more important to read the *New York Times* or *USA Today*. I can read the former without the latter but not the other way around, because here is where he has called me. Here is where he is working. Here is my post, my place, my life, his glory.

Word and Sacrament
Romantic realism explains why we give ourselves to the reading and preaching of God's Word along with the regular embrace of the bread and the cup.

Some romantically incant a biblical text as if magic lay buried in the page and ink. Others resign themselves to nothing more than the recitation of old words on a dead surface. But Paul the apostle confounds both views and speaks of a time instead in which preaching comes to the local place and its people, "not only in word, but also in power and in the Holy Spirit and with full conviction" (1 Thess. 1:5).

Some romantically exaggerate the voice as if holiness has a loud pitch, as if God speaks with a foghorn articulation that is laden with tremor or in contrast as only a timorous voice whispering shouts of glory. Others X-ray these vocal antics and are cynical of the song. "Voice," they say, "is nothing more." Voice is vocal-chord limited, empty. Voice is as cold as religion.

But Paul tells us otherwise. There are times in which the human voice speaks in all of its grandeur and frailty, but what the congregation hears is God himself speaking to them by and with this inked text and human voice. "When you received the word of God, which you heard from us, you accepted it not as the word of men but as what it really is, the word of God" (1 Thess. 2:13).

The Spirit takes up this Word, read and preached. The ordinary alphabet, the mundane voice, these giving life by the Spirit's breath, and ordinary people respond as if God is present. His Spirit in Jesus was speaking to them, and, with their flaws and limits, they actually "turned to God from idols to serve the living and true God, and to wait for his Son from heaven" (1 Thess. 1:9–10).

Likewise, the bread and cup "proclaim the Lord's death" (1 Cor. 11:26). Loaf and juice, wafer or wine, are nothing more than that. We bought them on sale around the corner. And yet he draws near here; uniquely we taste and see not only the dough and crushed grapes but the very goodness of the living Christ. Remembering him becomes greeting him. He meets us with real presence, while in faith we chew and swallow and pray. Death lurks here among the pieces. Life rises as we gather together. The body of the Lord is discerned here. Sacred we eat (1 Cor. 11:27–29).

What I am learning is that the romantic realist finds his or her way toward a long rhythm in a local place. Because by faith there is more to this ink and text, these varied human-preacher voices, these local people with their daily stories, this store-bought or stove-baked bread, and these cups of juice or cheap wine—there is more here, I am saying, than meets our eyes. God is here. The same old, same old has wings.

Homecoming

I remember myself as an adult in my first pastorate. There I was, sitting on that porch eating Mamaw's spice cake. A memory of myself as a boy comes back to me. After all, pastors were children and grandchildren once. I remember Mamaw calling out at suppertime. Sometimes she'd slip her feet into her plain canvas shoes of faded red and stand on the gravel drive just outside the carport. She'd hold the car door open with her left hand. With that right hand she'd lean down and knock the wind out of the steering wheel. In response to Mamaw's strength, the worn car horn would burst into gasping and thrust two goose-like wonks into the air.

At other times, she would speedily whack an old can with a wooden spoon. The spoon became a drumming instrument for making rhythm and causing loud clatter to rise into the neighborhood air at sunset.

My uncles and the neighborhood kids used the same can for the game I loved, "Kick the Can." I was young, and Mamaw forced her two sons to let me play. They were too young to be uncles but could do nothing about that. They had to let their nephew tag along.

I loved it. I felt older, like I belonged. It is remarkable the happiness an old plain can is able to offer a neighborhood of kids. This aspect of the can sometimes reminds me of people too. Equally remarkable is how useful the same can was in Mamaw's hands.

But the honking goose horn and the clanging soup can both fade in comparison to those times in my memory when Mamaw simply chose to use her own voice to call us home. Maybe we were down by the Guthries', hiding like soldiers in the bushes, or climbing trees. She would call my uncles' names first and then mine. "Bbbbbuuddd." "Aaaaddddddaaaammmm." "Zzzaaacckkkk."

Sometimes hearing Mamaw's voice calling on the wind annoyed me. Supper was ready. I wanted to play, not eat. I wanted to ramble through the neighborhood, not sit in my spot at that same old table. It was time to come home. And I refused. A foreshadowing of an obstinance in my heart that would harm both me and others in time.

But other times it stirred me to hear my name in Mamaw's voice calling at dusk. The older boys weren't always fair. They could make a game of me rather than inviting me to play one with them. I knew what it meant to hear her voice carrying our names at that time of night. Food was waiting. Rescue was certain. My heart could leap, my tears subside. It was time to come home. And I did.

I see in this scene a reminder of how Jesus calls any of us into this life and to this ministry. He called us on some street in a local place as those who belonged to somebody somewhere and whose family name had become our own. I was an Eswine and a Guernsey. I played games like "Kick the Can." I played Tonka trucks with my Uncle Adam. I drank pickle juice (thanks to my Uncle Bud). I heard my papaw finally speak of Jesus at the American Legion Hall in Henryville, Indiana. It was Thanksgiving (yes, it was).

I preached about Jesus at my mamaw's funeral. She died on Christmas Day. Songs I had written were played on the CD player as family and friends gathered. I was ordained to preach by the Great Lakes Presbytery. But I spoke of Jesus that day as Pauline's grandson, the broken son of Vern and Jan. I was that boy that Mamaw called "Charlie Brown" and a "dandy" (as she did others of her grandchildren). Afterward, we ate fried chicken and macaroni with tomatoes right there in the basement fellowship hall of the Henryville United Methodist Church.

Papaw died a little over three years later. In spite of the doctrinal convictions about women as pastors on the part of his grandson, Pastor Wilma had nurtured my old Papaw's young faith. She had tended to him faithfully and spoke wholeheartedly to him of Jesus. As we all sat in that funeral, she invited us to the same Savior that had pursued, found, and forgiven Bud, the same Savior that had answered Mamaw's prayers. More fried chicken followed, and then home.

What I'm trying to say is that life and ministry are an apprenticeship in Jesus in which, by his grace, he recovers our humanity, and for his glory he enables others to do the same. Bernanos had it right. "Grace is everywhere."[1]

Notes

Introduction
1. Carl Dennis, "Smaller," in *Unknown Friends* (New York: Penguin Poets, 2007), 16.

Chapter 1: Desire
1. Kathleen Graber, "Book Nine," Poetry Foundation website, accessed December 3, 2014, http://www.poetryfoundation.org/poem/241278.
2. Nathan Foster, *Wisdom Chasers: Finding My Father at 14,000 Feet* (Downers Grove, IL: InterVarsity, 2010), 41.

Chapter 2: Recovering Our Humanity
1. Gerard Manley Hopkins, "The Caged Skylark," in *Hopkins: Poems and Prose* (New York: Knopf, 1995), 17.

Chapter 4: Invisible
1. See, e.g., Matt. 8:4; 9:30; Mark 1:44; 3:12; 5:43; 7:36; Luke 8:56.
2. Eugene H. Peterson, *Under the Unpredictable Plant: An Exploration in Vocational Holiness* (Grand Rapids, MI: Eerdmans, 1994).

Chapter 5: Everywhere for All
1. Mary Oliver, *Writer's Almanac* website, accessed February 7, 2015, http://writersalmanac.publicradio.org/index.php?date=2011/09/10.
2. Matt. 13:54; Luke 2:4, 39, 51.
3. David Breashears and Audrey Salkeld, *Last Climb: The Legendary Everest Expeditions of George Mallory* (Washington, DC: National Geographic, 1999).
4. "After his disappearance on Everest close friends would say that Mallory had taken the decision to return with foreboding, telling them that what he would have to face this time would be "more like war than adventure" and that he doubted he would return. He knew that no one would criticize him if he refused to go, but he felt it a compulsion. It is impossible to say now whether these were more than fleeting moments of guilt at having to leave his wife Ruth yet again with all responsibility for their young children. Be that as it may, once on the road to Tibet again, Mallory was his usual

energetic self. "I feel strong for the battle," he wrote to Ruth from Base Camp, "but I know every ounce of strength will be wanted." "I have to look at it from the point of view of loyalty to the expedition," he wrote to his father as he vacillated, "and of carrying through a task begun." Audrey Salkeld, "Mallory," http://www.pbs.orgwgbh/nova/Everest/lost/mystery /Mallory.htm.
5. G. K. Chesterton, *Orthodoxy: The Romance of Faith* (New York: Image Books, 1990), 60.
6. Samuel Rutherford, *The Loveliness of Christ: Selections from Samuel Rutherford's Letters* (Edinburgh: Banner of Truth, 2007), 1.

Chapter 6: Fix It All

1. Richard M. Cohen, *Strong at the Broken Places: Voices of Illness, a Chorus of Hope* (New York: Harper, 2008), xvi.
2. Henri Nouwen, *The Wounded Healer: Ministry in Contemporary Society* (New York: Doubleday, 1979).
3. Mary Felstiner, *Out of Joint: A Private and Public Story of Arthritis* (Lincoln, NE: University of Nebraska Press, 2007), 89.
4. Ibid.

Chapter 7: Know It All

1. Not this dear man's real name.
2. Johann Wolfgang von Goethe, "The Sorcerer's Apprentice," http://www. germanstories.vcu.edu/goethe/zauber-e3.html.
3. Jonathan Edwards, "Some Thoughts Concerning the Present Revival of Religion in New England," in *The Works of Jonathan Edwards, vol. 4: The Great Awakening* (New Haven, CT: Yale University Press, 2009), np.
4. D. Martyn Lloyd-Jones, "Knowledge False and True," in *The Puritans: Their Origins and Successors* (Edinburgh: Banner of Truth, 1991), 28.
5. Steve Garber, "The Epistemology of Love," Washington Institute, http:// www.washingtonist.org/163/the-epistemology-of-love/, 2.
6. Augustine, *On Christian Teaching,* Oxford World's Classics, trans. R. P. H. Green (New York: Oxford University Press, 1997), 27.

Chapter 8: Immediacy

1. Eugene Peterson, "Spirituality for All the Wrong Reasons," *Christianity Today,* March 2005, http://www.christianitytoday.com/CT/2005/March/26.42. html?start=y.

Chapter 9: A New Ambition

1. St. John of the Cross, *Dark Night of the Soul* (New York: Doubleday, 1999).
2. John Calvin, "Commentary on James 1:19–21," in *Commentaries on the Catholic Epistles,* trans. John Owen, Christian Classics Ethereal Library, accessed April 28, 2015, http://www.ccel.org/ccel/calvin/calcom45.vi.ii.vi .html?scrBook=Jas&scrCh=1&scrV=19#vi.ii.vi-p9.1.

3. See my *Preaching to a Post-Everything World: Crafting Biblical Sermons That Connect with Our Culture* (Grand Rapids, MI: Baker, 2008); and *Kindled Fire: How the Methods of C. H. Spurgeon Can Help Your Preaching* (Ross-shire, UK: Mentor, 2006).
4. Henri Nouwen, *The Way of the Heart: Connecting with God Through Prayer, Wisdom, and Silence* (New York: Ballantine, 1981), 48.
5. Richard Foster, *Celebration of Discipline: The Path to Spiritual Growth* (New York: HarperSanFrancisco, 1988), 86.
6. Dietrich Bonhoeffer, *Life Together: The Classic Exploration of Christian Community* (New York: HarperSanFrancisco, 1988), 84–85.
7. Ibid., 85.
8. William Stafford, "Malheur Before Dawn," in *Even in Quiet Places* (Lewiston, ID: Confluence Press, 1996), 49.
9. Matthew Henry, *A Discourse Concerning Meekness and Quietness of Spirit*, in *The Complete Works of Matthew Henry* (Grand Rapids, MI: Baker, 1997), 133.
10. Ibid., 109.
11. Ibid., 134.
12. Ibid.
13. Ibid., 107.
14. Ibid., 127.
15. Michael A. Eaton, *Ecclesiastes*, Tyndale Old Testament Commentaries (Downers Grove, IL: InterVarsity, 2009), 150.
16. Charles Spurgeon, *Lectures to My Students* (Grand Rapids, MI: Zondervan, 1954), 51.
17. John Calvin, *Institutes of the Christian Religion*, trans. Ford Lewis Battles (Philadelphia: Westminster, 1960), 2.3.10.
18. Ibid.
19. John Cassian, *Conferences: The Classics of Western Spirituality*, trans. Colm Luibheid (New York: Paulist Press, 1985), 158.
20. Ibid.
21. Ibid.
22. Francis Schaeffer, *No Little People* (Wheaton, IL: Crossway, 2003), 29.
23. Richard Baxter, *Converse with God in Solitude* (New York: C. Wells, 1833), 153–54.
24. Ibid., 100–101.

Chapter 10: Beholding God

1. Adapted from Henri Nouwen, *Spiritual Direction: Wisdom for the Long Walk of Faith* (New York: HarperCollins, 2006), 4.
2. Beholding can also ask God to pause and grow fixedly attentive to a longing of our heart or to a commitment or condition of our lives (Pss. 17:2; 39:5; 84:9; 119:40).
3. M. Craig Barnes, *The Pastor as Minor Poet: Texts and Subtexts in the Ministerial Life* (Grand Rapids, MI: Eerdmans, 2009), 22.

4. E. E. Cummings, "Walking on Water."
5. John Calvin, *Instruction in Faith* (Louisville, KY: Westminster, 1992), 21.
6. Leighton Ford, "Wholly and Holy Listening," unpublished paper, Mentoring Gathering (May 2014), 5.
7. Calvin, *Instruction in Faith*, 57.
8. For a full list of prayers in the Bible, see Herbert Lockyer, *All the Prayers of the Bible*, http://gospelpedlar.com/articles/Christian%20Life/Prayer.pdf.
9. See, e.g., Psalms 3; 7; 18; 30; 34; 52; 54; 56; 57; 59; 63.
10. Calvin, *Instruction in Faith*, 57 (emphasis added).
11. Even if the imaginary conversation has a positive end in mind, such as the prodigal son's imagined conversation with his father, our one-sided conversation is a poor substitute for psalm making. It enables us to wrongly guess how another might respond. We inadvertently project upon them what isn't true at all. The son, for example, could only imagine his father's disdain, his being no longer a son but a slave (Luke 15:18–19).
12. Zack Eswine, *Preaching to a Post-Everything World* (Grand Rapids, MI: Baker, 2008) and *Kindled Fire: How the Preaching Methods of C. H. Spurgeon Can Help Your Preaching* (Ross-shire, UK: Christian Focus, 2003).
13. Archibald Alexander, *Thoughts on Religious Experience* (1844; repr. Edinburgh: Banner of Truth, 1989), 162.
14. Ibid.
15. Richard Baxter, *A Christian Directory*, vol. 1, *Christian Ethics* (1846; repr. Morgan, PA: Soli Deo Gloria, 1996), 477.
16. *The Sayings of the Desert Fathers*, trans. Benedicta Ward (Kalamazoo, MI: Cistercian, 1984), 7.
17. Baxter, *A Christian Directory*, 478.
18. John Calvin, *Institutes of the Christian Religion*, trans. Ford Lewis Battles (Philadelphia: Westminster, 1960), 1.6.3.

Chapter 11: Finding Our Pace
1. For more on this see *Dictionary of Biblical Imagery*, ed. Leland Ryken, James C. Wilhoit, and Tremper Longman III (Downers Grove, IL: InterVarsity, 1998).
2. Kathleen Norris, *Acedia and Me: A Marriage, Monks, and a Writer's Life* (New York: Riverhead, 2008), *xiv*.
3. Nathan Foster, *Wisdom Chaser: Finding My Father at 14,000 Feet* (Downers Grove, IL: InterVarsity, 2010), 34.

Chapter 13: Care for the Sinner
1. See Rom. 16:16; 1 Cor. 16:20; 2 Cor. 13:12; 1 Thess. 5:26.

Chapter 14: Local Knowledge
1. Annie Dillard, *Teaching a Stone to Talk: Expeditions and Encounters* (New York: HarperPerennial, 1992), 36–39.

2. Wendell Berry, *The Art of the Commonplace: The Agrarian Essays of Wendell Berry* (Berkeley, CA: Counterpoint Press, 2002), 11.
3. Robert Flayhart, *Gospel-Centered Mentoring*, DMin dissertation, Covenant Theological Seminary, 2001.

Chapter 15: Leadership
1. C. S. Lewis, "The Inner Ring," in *The Weight of Glory* (New York: HarperCollins, 2001), 150.
2. Ibid., 145.
3. Ibid., 149.

Chapter 16: Romantic Realism
1. Georges Bernanos, *The Diary of a Country Priest* (New York: Knoll & Graff, 2004), 298.

General Index

General Index

portions as a day of rest, 182–83. *See also* day, the, four portions of

David, 100

day, the, four portions of, 172–73; and God as our portion, 173, 174; as one portion draws to a close, pause and look back before you start the new portion, 180; as portions large enough for your attention and small enough to manage, 180–82. *See also the specific portions (morning, noon, evening, the night watches)*

Deborah, 246, 247

decision making: asking if this is the right thing, 236–38; asking if this is the right time, 240–41; asking what is the right way to do this, 239–40; "Board Room" decision making, 230; and delegating the dreaming, 237–39; "Emergency Room" decision making, 230

defensiveness, 95–96; emotional blasting, 96–97; record keeping, 96–97

demons: identification of Jesus by, 76; overpowering of Paul's apprentices by, 104–5

Dennis, Carl, 13

desire, 19–20; desire for greatness as Jesus defines it, 29; desire for the loveliness of Jesus himself, 31; desiring to do a great thing for God, 21–23; Jesus's posing of the question of desire ("What do you want me to do for you?"), 29–31; and pastoral vocation, 18–19

devotions. *See* quiet time

DiCamillo, Kate, 245

Dillard, Annie, 214–15

disciples, the (of Jesus): Jesus's training of, 64–65; "little t" theologies of, 46–47. *See also* James and John; Judas; Matthew; Peter

dreams, 179–80; beholding the fruit of a dream, 165–66; as providential, 179; the sources of dreams (from us, from Satan, or from God), 179

Eaton, Michael A., 143

Edwards, Jonathan, 106

Elijah, 246

Esau, 161

Eswine, Zack: advice of to parents whose child disliked God, 57–58; advice of to would-be pastors ("Jonathan Edwards farted"), 34–35, 43; books of on the ministry of the Word, 258n12; books of on preaching and evangelism, 257n3; and Caleb's request that he fix the broken moon, 108–9; conversations of with a young pastor, 23–25; dealing with people leaving his church, 119–20, 121–22, 128–30; desire of for ministry as an eight-year-old, 20; dizzy spells of, 118; dream of about preaching on Psalm 138, 154–66; failed marriage of, 22–23, 202; hometown of (Henryville, Indiana), 75–76; interview of with a church search committee, 226–28; as a man with fists and fears, 47–48; and Mamaw's funeral, 252; memories of Mamaw, 219–20, 251–52; misplaced desire of (for finding an epic moment), 17–19, 20–23; Papaw's advice to ("Just taking one day at a time"), 172; and Papaw's funeral, 252–53; and Papaw's return to the faith, 54–55; and Papaw's way of seeing the world, 45–46, 49; and Pat's funeral, 191–94; poetry of, 16, 49, 80, 245; preaching barefoot, 43; and the temptation of being everywhere for all, 73–74; "vaccine" of against knowledge in sorts, 110; "Why I'm what some people call 'a Calvinist,'" 52

evening, 176–77; and hospitality, 176; Jesus in the evening, 177; in the Psalms, 176; timeframe of, 173

exiles, in Babylonia, 83–84; obstacles confronted by, 84; the two different kinds of preachers giving sermons to them, 83

faith, 97, 196; the prayer of faith, 195–97

Felstiner, Mary, 101–2

Flayhart, Robert, on the Waltz of the Gospel rubric, 223

Ford, Leighton, 156

forgiveness, 109, 206, 231
Foster, Nathan, 21, 183–84
Foster, Richard, 21, 140

Garber, Steve, 110
Gideon, 246, 247
God: grace of, 67; interrupting God, 138–39, 149; as our portion, 173, 174; remembrance of, 61–62; slowness of, 121
godly grief, 207; godly grief leads the person back to a fresh acquaintance with the provisions of salvation, 207; godly grief produces repentance, 207; godly grief purposes to send regret away, 207
Goethe, Johann Wolfgang von, 104
Graber, Kathleen, 19

Hammarskjöld, Dag, 169
Hansen, David, 45
haste, 28, 120–22; as "feeling late" or "thinking we have to run," 121; as no friend to desire, 28–29; as part of the air we breathe, 121
Henry, Matthew, 141–42
Herod, 62–63, 99
heroes, unlikely, 246–47; heroes who never receive the limelight of their generation, 246; heroic moments are heavenly but not heaven, 246–47; heroic moments have as their aim the recovery of the ordinary, 247; sometimes the aid of God is found in provision of an ordinary grain or an ordinary friend, 247
Hopkins, Gerard Manley, 37
hospitality. *See* hospitable presence
hospitable presence, 149, 151, 152, 176
humility, 42, 113

imaginary conversations, 161
immediacy. *See* haste
impatience, 28, 124–25; impatient knowledge, 112–13; impatient preaching, 127
instant gratification. *See* haste

James and John: desire of for greatness, 29–30; wanting to kill Samaritans in God's name, 47, 101
Jeremiah, 83
Jesus: active pursuit of decision making by, 240; the "cannots" of Jesus's teaching, 96–97; as a carpenter in Nazareth, 77, 82, 87; as a crossroads, 26; crucifixion and resurrection of, 247; daily routine of, 63–64; death of at noon, 175–76; the demons' identification of, 76; fame-shyness of, 60–62; as the Good Shepherd, 114; harsh words of for the ministry leaders of his day, 100; how Jesus handled Peter's getting things wrong, 111–12; Jesus in the evening, 177; Jesus in the morning, 173, 174; Jesus at noon, 175, 175–76; Jesus's family members' response to his ministry, 53–54; Jesus's hometown's response to his ministry, 52; Jesus's inversion of the narratives around which we map the world, 51; Jesus's limiting of himself and inhabiting a locality on earth, 76–77; Jesus's response to James and John's request, 30; Jesus's sense of place, 76–77; Jesus's training of the disciples for ministry, 64–65; Jesus's way of strategic networking in the Gospel of Luke (invisible people, invisible prayers), 62–64; Jesus's "Woe!" to those who misuse the key of knowledge, 107; on patience, 127; as the poor wise man of Ecclesiastes 9, 148; as the returning shepherd, 85; silence of, 140; as the suffering servant, 152; temptation of, 162–63; and the touching of the sick, 190–91; what Jesus says that knowing is, 114–15
Job's friends: doctrinal correctness of, 99–100; sitting in the ashes with Job, 93
John the Baptist: confession of ("I am not the Christ"), 37; confusion of about Jesus's ministry, 62
Jonah, 100
Judas, 212

ministry, and facing the temptation to fix it all: mounting an offense when no match is ours to win, 101–2; and the reality that ministry in Jesus's name involves life lived among brokenness, 89–90; recognizing that we are winsome harmers, 99–101; recognizing that we cannot do everything that needs to be done, 99; recognizing that we cannot fix the absence of peace the way people often want us to, 98–99; recognizing that we cannot fix the "inconsolable things," 96–97; recognizing that we have no power to produce the "increasing things," 97

ministry, and invisibility: and being already discovered, 68–69; the fame-shyness of Jesus, 60–62; humdrum work, 57–59; invisible people, invisible prayers, 62–64; trusting Jesus more than appearances, 67–68

ministry, and leaving home: and family members' responses, 52–54; men with fists and fears, 47–48; the mentoring we bring with us ("Big T" and "little t" theologies), 46–47; race in conversation, 50–51; women with bodies, 48–50

ministry, and recovering our humanity, 35–36; being human ("preaching barefoot"), 41–43; and the confession "I am not the Christ," 35–36; human locality, 38–39; human physicality, 36–37; preparing our bodily senses for ministry, 37–38; seeing people, 40–41

ministry, and using strategies other than the gospel to fix all the broken things 89–90; defensiveness, 95–96; fear and intimidation, 95; multiplying words, 91–92; raising our voices and pointing our fingers, 93–95; throwing Bible words about, 92–93

morning, 173–74, 176; Jesus in the morning, 173, 174; in the Psalms, 173, 173–74; as the time of grace, 174; timeframe of, 173

Moses, 100

Muir, Edwin, 213

Naomi, 248

night watches, the, 177–79; and dreams, 179–80; as a place of solitude, 178; in the Psalms, 178, 178–79; timeframe of, 173

Noah, 100

noon, 174–76, 176; Jesus at noon, 175, 175–76; the "noon-day demon," 175; in the Psalms, 174–75; timeframe of, 173

Norris, Kathleen, 175

Nouwen, Henri, 139, 153; on the "wounded healer," 99

Oliver, Mary, 74

parable of the good Samaritan, the religious leaders in, 96, 100

parable of the prodigal son: the elder brother in, 100; the prodigal son's imagined conversation with his father in, 258n11

parable of two church planters, 32

pastoral care of the sick, 28, 187–88; calling for the elders to pray, 194–95; confession of the true need for forgiveness, 197–98; funerals, 191–94; and gospel touch, 188–90; Jesus and the touching of the sick, 190–91; letting a sinner be to the church as a "Gentile and tax collector," 202–4; the prayer of faith, 195–97

pastoral care of the sinner, 199–200; church discipline and sin, 200; discerning sin from a limit or an accident, 210–11; discerning sorrow for sin ("godly grief" versus self-generated grief), 207–8; Paul's advice on where to start, 208–10; relating to the hardened, 200–201; relating to the softened, 204–6; starting with ourselves, 201–2

pastors: as change agents in God's hands for the good of congregations, 225–26; the pastor's daily life as mundane, invisible, uncontrollable, and unfinished, 58–59; as servants, 30; as shepherds, 75, 218, 231; the two main fears of pastors (people will leave; they will be judged as failures),

Scripture Index